Facial Reconstruction for Artists

Facial Reconstruction
for Artists

A Guide to Producing Realistic Faces and Expressions Using
Techniques of Facial Reconstruction

Jan Flood

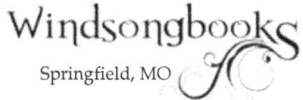

Windsongbooks
Springfield, MO

Library of Congress Control Number: 2010905449
ISBN: 978-0-578-05427-8

Publisher's Cataloging-in-Publication data

Flood, Jan.
    Facial reconstruction for artists : a guide to producing realistic faces and expressions using techniques of facial reconstruction / Jan Flood.
    p. cm.
    ISBN 978-0-578-05427-8
    Includes bibliographical references.
1. Face in art. 2. Drawing --Technique --Handbooks, manuals, etc. 3. Drawing --Technique. 4. Sculpture --Handbooks, manuals, etc. 5. Facial reconstruction (Anthropology) -- Handbooks, manuals, etc. 6. Anatomy, Artistic. I. Title.

NC770 .F46 2010
743.4/9--dc22   2010905449

Edited by JoAnna Tauscher Birdsall, Ed.D
Cover Design by Anna Farrand
Cover Model Jennifer Flood
Printed and bound in the United States of America on archival quality paper

To Hal, who has always been the wind beneath my wings

"I can fly higher than an eagle,
'cause you are the wind beneath my wings."

Wind Beneath My Wings
Henley/Silbar (1982)

Acknowledgements

This has not been a solitary journey. It isn't possible to write a book like this without the generous spirit of others. Over the years, I learned a great deal from my teachers, mentors and, as an instructor, I also learned from my students.

Like many kids growing up during those years we played cowboy and Indians, searched for arrowheads and fossils. My interest grew into more than play and as I got older, I began to read and study more about the lives of the people who lived before us. I soon discovered the wealth of information available in public libraries and started searching for books on these subjects.

Later, I was able to study the fields of Archeology and Anthropology in school. When the internet became available it opened up a whole new world of information, research publications, anthropology projects, university materials and pictures of places and things I'd only read about. I was able to increase my knowledge through books and papers written by working anthropologists. I researched, studied, and absorbed a great deal of information. As I sorted and sifted through all the materials, I discovered my desire to focus on forensic anthropology.

I want to thank Forensic Anthropologist, Dr. George Gill for his many years of work in this field as well as his generous sharing of his findings. Many thanks also go to Dr. Stanley Rhine for his belief that "Data are of no use if sequestered away". I would like to acknowledge Dr. Ted Rathbun for his help and advice. Dr. Rhine and Dr. Rathbun are also Forensic Anthropologists and all three men have been honored in their field. Thanks to Mary Manhein, Director of the Louisiana State University FACES Laboratory, and Dr. Tanya Peckmann for sharing their research on Tissue Depths. A special thank you to Betty Pat. Gatliff, who was the catalyst for turning my interest in Facial Reconstruction into a passion. I appreciate all of the research that has been made available and have acknowledged and credited researchers and/or original authors where I have known them. To the best of my ability, I documented all the information and cross-referenced it with verifiable sources. For any errors, I take full responsibility.

In addition to the above, I owe a debt of gratitude to my family and friends who have helped make this book possible. They encouraged me to begin this project and were still with me when I felt like quitting. Other individuals include the librarians who were invaluable with their help obtaining books and research materials. Dr. Jo Anna Birdsall, for her editing skills; Janet Flood, for reading and evaluating, the text for clarity. Anna Farrand for the cover design, Maggie Pagratis for her work on the interior design, Jennifer Flood and Christina Flood for serving as models, Lisa VerPloeg for sharing her family photos, and William Birdsall for believing I can do anything. Victoria Contreras Flores, for her work on the website Artnatomia.net and generously sharing it with others. There are many other individuals who offered advice and guidance along the way and no matter how small their contribution, it all made a difference. All of you share in any success of this book.

Most importantly, my love and appreciation go to my husband who put up with me the entire year while I worked on this book. He is my best friend, advisor, and source of strength. Not only did he support my decision to write this book, he took the time to read and review it multiple times. When I was too involved to stop and cook meals, he filled in and kept me going. From the day I met him, he has truly been the wind beneath my wings.

What Jan's Students Are Saying

"...I have to say Jan that I was extremely impressed with your teaching style, materials, and helpful suggestions. I have already recommended your class to many other artists who I am in contact with and have told many groups about your class as well. Totally wonderful class. Wonderfully done! My kudos to you for a great sculpting experience." Karen R.

"...I find that I am looking at people differently and my sculpting is showing marked improvement. I truly enjoyed taking the on line class. It fit my needs very well." Ginny B.

"...I'm almost ready to send you a picture of my gal as soon as I finish her hair. I must say, she turned out pretty and is one of the best heads I have done. The information you provided really helped me... I really think I've improved. I could have made her ears smaller, but overall I'm really happy. I must say that I've taken other classes that were much more expensive and drawn out and didn't learn nearly as much as I have from you. Thank you so much! I'm looking forward to your next class on an Asian skull." Kathleen K.

"...Thank you Jan, I learned a lot in this class and enjoyed very much. Thanks every one for all your comments from which I also solved many doubts." "Good luck to everyone." Roberto F.

"...The class did exceed my expectations; I certainly didn't expect such good results, especially since it was my first time." Susanna M.

"...When I worked on my last portrait I made sure to have a skull in front of me. I think it turned out better than anything I'd sculpted so far." Elizabeth B.

"...I love to study the faces and bone structure ...in the generations...as the oldest member of our family. I am the one who remembers the ones who came from the "old country" Norway & Ireland (Scots)...and their very strong features...I want my faces to be expressive and how I want them to be ...not how they turn out by accident ." Sandee E.

"...I truly enjoyed taking the on line class. It fit my needs very well. I hope to do this kind of training in the future." Anne S.

"...Thank you for this outstanding class. I have thoroughly enjoyed it & learned heaps. Now to apply it to my dolls." Sarah M.

"...Just read through this lesson. Wow, it is beautifully written and so easy to follow. I have been unhappy with the eyes I sculpt ever since I saw the work of another artist whose day job was in ophthalmology. Says a lot for knowing your anatomy, LOL. I'm sure I'll have more questions, but thanks so much for this good information." Kathi K.

"...The materials were exactly what was needed for the class. The pace was good, it gave plenty of time to read our notes and get the sculpt done, even with our busy lives. Very helpful". Cathy P.

"The lessons are the best I've ever seen. You are a doll for offering so much information. Thanks." Liz L.

"...Jan thanks a million for the class and your suggestions; everything has been more than worth taking the class." Donna W.

"...Thank you, Jan, for a wonderful class. I learned a great deal. I don't look at faces the same way anymore. I now see the skull and it is very helpful in sculpting faces." Eva W.

"...Your instructions made forming the shape of the foil head armature a lot better and sculpting was much easier than before. Thank you. I really learned quite a bit from your class." Ted M.

Contents

Preface

Artists often stand in front of their finished sculpture and wonder why it doesn't look like the image they had in their head. When that happens, it's like finding yourself at the end of a dead end road and wondering where you made a wrong turn. If you're reading this book most likely your goal is to produce more realistic or life-like faces, based on realistic bone and muscle structure. If it seems like a lot of work, you might take a hint from Michelangelo.

"If people knew how hard I worked to get my mastery, it wouldn't seem so wonderful at all." Michelangelo

If an artist like Michelangelo had to work this hard to achieve his goals, who are we to do less? Much as an architect has to study many years to learn the details necessary to construct a safe building so must the artist learn his craft. The skull creates the architectural form of the head and provides the basic structure for the face. Your first step, then, is developing a good knowledge of the framework. Sculpting from the inside out is beginning with the framework, adding the muscles, then the soft tissue. This also means there will be much less work when you reach the final stage of sculpting. You won't have to sculpt every bone and muscle every time, but knowing the locations will allow you to keep the framework in mind as you sculpt. Building your head this way rather than rushing to get the features on will eliminate a lot frustration, plus reward you with a more polished and professional figure. Bruno Lucchesi, Lisa Lichtenfels and George Stuart create their pieces from the inside out. They use different mediums; however, all three produce remarkable, lifelike creations.

Even as a kid, I loved Archeology and Anthropology. I studied both subjects in school and continued to pursue my interest in the following years. As my interest in Forensic Anthropology grew, I found myself combining this with my sculpting, focusing on Forensic Sculpting (Facial Reconstruction). I started searching for information on the subject and eventually found a book, purchased a study skull and started practicing. When I had the opportunity to study with Betty Pat. Gatliff, one of the foremost American Forensic Sculptors, I immediately said yes and will always appreciate her support and encouragement.

It's important to note, this book is not meant to be a complete study of forensic facial reconstruction, anatomy or even sculpting. My goal is to provide you with information that will help you develop your own skills, enhance your talents, and learn those realistic details that will add believability to your figures. To again quote Michelangelo, "The greater danger for most of us lies not in setting our aim too high and falling short; but in setting our aim too low, and achieving our mark."

Introduction to Facial Reconstruction

Traditional artists strive to produce beautiful and/or inspiring art. The goal of a Forensic Artist, on the other hand, is to produce a likeness of an individual that might lead to recognition. Using the skull as a base for sculpting, the forensic artist uses various skeletal markers and identifiers to reconstruct the face. Facial Reconstruction isn't a new science, but it came into its own in the early 1980's when law enforcement began using it to help establish identities of victims.

Occasionally you hear in the news of a hunter out in the woods who discovers a human skeleton that may have been there for years. There are no items with the body that will help establish identity, and law enforcement has no information or leads to go on. If officers suspect this was a homicide, it is important to find out who the victim was before they can begin to solve the crime. A Forensic Anthropologist will study the bones and obtain as much information from them as possible. When other means of identification have failed, they may call in a Forensic Artist to do a reconstruction on the skull.

Once completed, they will have a 3-dimensional idea of what the individual might have looked like in life. Circulating photos of the reconstruction through the media often leads to someone recognizing the individual and coming forward.

In another scenario, a farmer finds an intact skull in his pasture. After a thorough examination, authorities determine it is from a much earlier time. To get an idea of what this early human may have looked like a forensic artist may be asked to prepare a facial reconstruction. You will often see these in museum displays that portray early humans. As a result, you will often hear that facial reconstruction is a blending of art and science.

Museums use trained artists to assist in exhibitions as well as archeological projects. A forensic artist may work on genealogy projects to help identify individuals and get an idea of what they looked like in the time they lived. Other forensic artists volunteer their time and talents to organizations such as *Project EDAN – Everyone Deserves a Name,* and *The Doe Network.* Both organizations are dedicated to helping establish identities and/or assist law enforcement in locating missing individuals.

On the following page, I have included an excerpt from the Rapa Nui Journal, The Journal of the Easter Island Foundation. The paper, *Facial Features of the Ancient Rapa Nui,* was presented by Sharon Long and George Gill. It casts more light on the importance of facial reconstruction in areas other than identification of skeletal remains.

Human osteological research was a part of the 1987-88, KonTiki Expedition to Easter Island. As part of this research, casts were made from six well-preserved skulls, three males, and three females. The original remains are housed within the collection of the Sebastian Englert Museum on Easter Island, and the University of Minnesota. The casts and molds are with the Department of Anthropology, University of Wyoming.

As part of a museum enhancement project for the Sebastian Englert Museum, facial reconstructions were done on two of the six casts, one male, and one female. In 1989 the reconstructed faces were taken back to Easter Island and put on display at the Museum.

Sharon Long, University of Wyoming, approached the reconstructions in much the same way a reconstruction is created for an unidentified victim in a crime situation. She used the American method of cutting long erasers to the exact length in millimeters and glued them to the skull casts, at the specifically designated points on the tissue depth charts (Rhine and Moore 1982). The clay was applied in strips to the depth of each marker. Care was taken to keep the marker in sight at all times and to apply the clay evenly. Once the surface was filled in with clay, she began aging the skin surface to the estimated age at death. Extreme accuracy is important in a scientific setting. Skulls of two previous forensic cases were obtained. In both instances, positive identifications were attained and photographs available. Working with these fulfilled their hopes of achieving a true to life reconstruction that was also aesthetically pleasing.

During the first week of display, three local Rapa Nui men visiting the museum showed a keen interest in the reconstructed face of the prehistoric Easter Island male. Each one expressed the belief that there was a recognizable resemblance between this prehistoric face and existing family members living on Easter Island today. The family was that of Heri Veri. The museum began a search of the location of the original excavation in 1978, and a search of the genealogical records from Easter Island. Among the modern families descended from the Miru lineage was one listed as Heri Veri.

Later, they met with the male members of the Heri Veri family and were able to take photographs. The obvious resemblance between the face reconstructed on the ancient Miru male and the faces of living descendants is noteworthy. For this to happen required not only an accurate application of facial reconstruction techniques, but also a preservation of facial features for centuries, within a prominent Easter Island lineage. The heredity line had to endure the incredible decimation of the Easter Island population during the 19th century from disease and slave raids.   (Rapa Nui Journal Vol 11(2) June 1997 p 72-74)

Study Skulls

A study skull is a necessary item if you are serious about learning to sculpt realistic heads and faces. There are artists who have an innate ability to look at someone and sculpt him or her with no preliminary work. I would be willing to bet, however, that even those artists spent some time learning and studying to improve their work. Famous artists spent most of their lives working at their craft, looking for ways to improve.

It is often hard for artists to envision the shape of a skull from all angles. This is one area where a picture will not have the same benefit. No matter how you look at it or turn it around, it will always be a flat picture. The value in a study skull is in being able to see not only the size and shape of the bones, but how they connect to form the skull. Study skulls are casts made from human skulls. They may be plastic, resin or other material and come in a wide range of prices. You can get a plastic skull for around $50 or spend more for a very realistic one. Remember, these are an investment in yourself. You can practice with it and use it for reference for many years. Get one in the price range you are comfortable with, you can always purchase a better one later.

The price of a study skull also depends on your choice of gender and race. The more specific you are the more you can expect to pay. The skull used in the demonstration in this book is from Bone Clones Inc. I've purchased from them a number of times and have always been very pleased. The skulls shown in Part Two, Ethnic Differences, are from their catalog and used with their permission. There are a number of good companies providing study skulls in a variety of prices. A Google search for study skulls will return many websites and you can even find them on e-bay. I've listed a few in the Reference Section to get you started. Spend the necessary time to review several sites prior to purchasing one. Everything changes, so a site that has good specimens one year may carry something different the next. In addition, some companies sell skulls that are produced by another company so you might see different prices for the same skull. Read all the information and e-mail the company if you have questions.

Once you have your study skull, you will need to mount it on a stand. Some skulls come mounted on their own stand and I've provided instructions to make the stand I use. You might prefer a different type of stand, it's your choice. Whichever method you use to hold the skull, it needs to be at your eye level while you are sculpting. You can use books or other sturdy items to raise it to eye level. I am able to raise and lower the sculpting stand I use so I can sculpt standing up or sitting down. They are available in art supply stores.

Part One

Intelligent Observation

Intelligent Observation

*T*his first part will introduce you to observation, Intelligent Observation. We are always observing family, friends, and co-workers in endless situations, but if you believe we all see the same thing, just talk to a police officer. With their experience interviewing witnesses, they will tell you that several witnesses, who observe the same incident, will often give different information as to what they saw. Sometimes it is radically different information depending on their point of view and their powers of observation. Intelligent observation for an artist requires some basic knowledge of anatomy to evaluate the differences you see.

We've all heard the three rules of real estate: "location, location, location". Realtors use this saying to remind themselves that the value of the location is determined first, before other options are considered. Intelligent observation is as important to an artist as location is to a realtor. As you become aware of the value of observation, your ability to recognize individual differences will increase. As you begin to apply this, you will see an improvement in your work.

If you always do what you've always done, you'll always get what you've always got. This saying is attributed to several people, but is true for many things in life, and is especially true if you work from memory. The result will be what your brain has stored in memory, not necessarily how it really is. Your brain learns to expect that features will always fall in a certain place. We see the face as whole, not individual details.

Let's do a quick exercise to get started. On a sheet of paper, draw a rose from memory. Include the stem and leaves. Check your drawing against the pictures (Figures 1-1 and 1-2). How close was your drawing to the picture? Draw the rose again, using the pictures as a guide. The roses are from my own garden. The open rose is a deep, dark red and the bud, a deep pink. Both are very fragrant. Examine the shape of the individual petals. Each one wraps around the neighboring one in a circular pattern and connects to the base. The green leaves at the base of the rose are Sepals. They protect the flower until it blooms, then open as the petals open. The cane (or stem) has leaves, thorns and bud eyes.

Roses

Figure 1-1

The center petals form a tight bud. Each individual petal wraps around its neighbor to form a circular pattern.

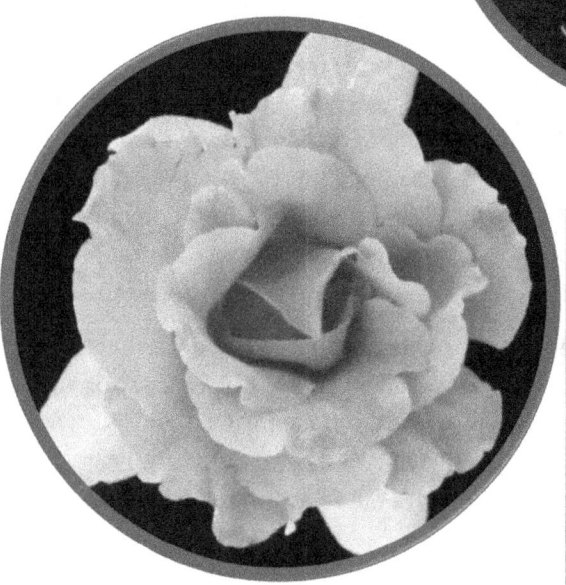

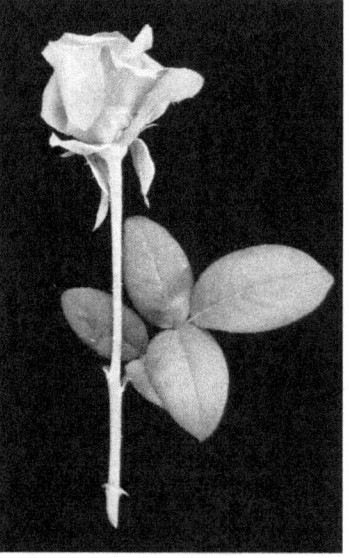

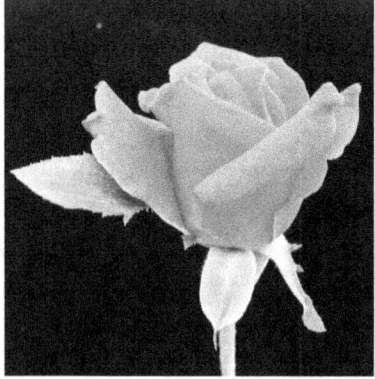

The green Sepals protect the flower until the petals begin to open, then opens with them.

Petals and Leaves
Figure 1-2

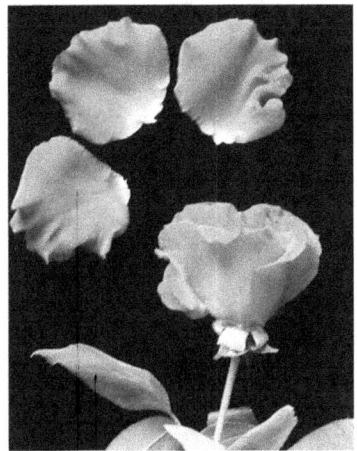

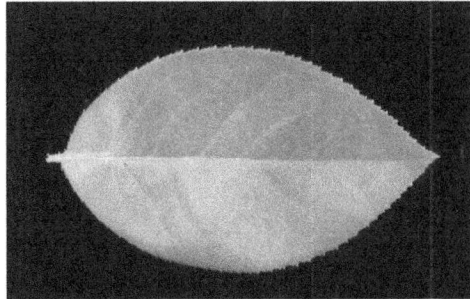

The center vein is indented on the front side of a leaf.

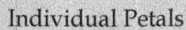

Individual Petals

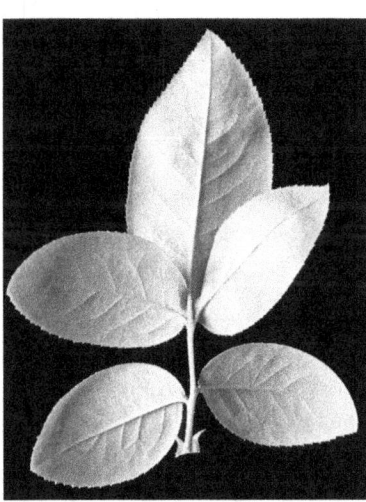

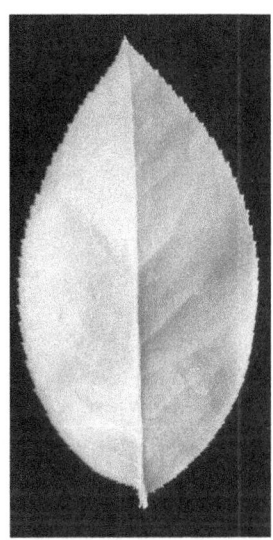

The prominent center vein is raised on the back side of a leaf.

Rose leaves have fine serrated edges and grow in pairs on opposite sides of the stem with one end leaf.

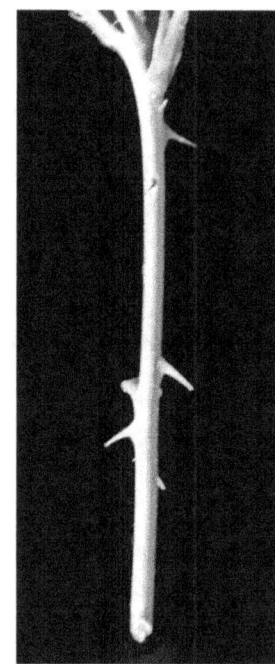

If asked, would you say the thorns on a rose grow up, or down? Did you say up? The photo right (Figure 1-3), clearly shows the thorns growing down.

Figure 1-3

I love roses. They are a lot of work to grow but the pleasure they give makes it worth the trouble. I've read there are over 6,500 varieties of roses - including Grandiflora roses, Hybrid Tea roses, old roses, wild roses, miniature roses and climbing roses, to name just a few. If you saw every one of the 6,500 varieties, you would always recognize each one as a rose. Even though they are different sizes, shapes and colors, our brain is programmed to recognize a rose. Faces are like this. There are infinite variations on the size and shape of individual features. Our brain stores a template of an average face. When we see someone we know, the brain instantly compares the face to the template. A person's distinct and unique variations allow our brain to recognize them as different individuals. Did you know the brain recognizes faces in a vertical alignment? Seen upside down they are much harder to recognize. Try it sometime. You can use this same exercise to develop your powers of observation with faces. On a sheet of paper, draw a face from memory including the features. Draw the face a second time using a picture or someone who is willing to model for you. Take the time to study the individual features. Where do the eyebrows begin? How are the upper and lower eyelids shaped? Where does the nose begin and end? Observe several different people close to you and note the similarities and differences. A child draws very basic shapes as she sees them (Figure 1-4). Often that's what we get when we draw from memory; a simplified form with all the right parts but lacking the fine details.

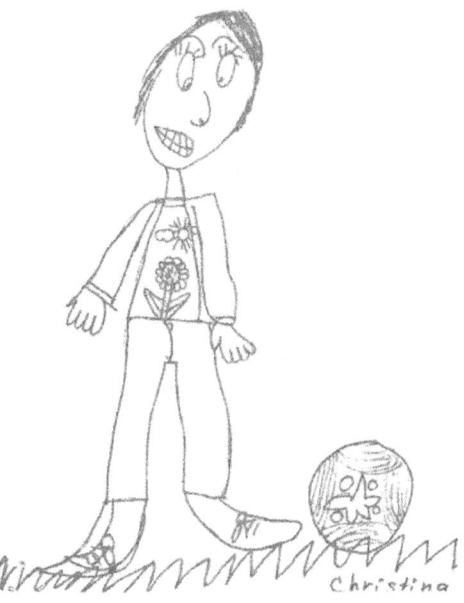

Figure 1-4
Original drawing by Christina Flood, age 5 yrs

An exercise Betty Edwards teaches in her book, *Drawing on the Right Side of the Brain* (1979) is to choose a picture, turn it upside down and draw what you see, not what you think it should look like. Try this for yourself. Surprisingly, when you turn it around it will be a fairly good drawing consistent with the original picture. This forces you to use a different part of your brain.

This practice is based on the research of Roger Sperry, Ph.D. (1913-1994) that led to his Nobel Peace Prize in Medicine (1981). Sperry's research showed that the brain is divided into two major parts or hemispheres. The right brain and the left brain. His research also identified that each part of the brain specializes in its own style of thinking and has different capabilities. A person who is said to be "left-brained" is more logical, analytical, and objective. A person who is "right-brained" is thought to be more intuitive, thoughtful, and creative. One of the things that make the left-brain powerful is the ability to use common "symbols" or "templates" to speed up the thought processes. The left side is very good at taking a small bit of information and using it to represent the whole. Remember the 6,500 varieties of roses? We always recognize them as roses. We know a wheel is round so we will always see an object portrayed as a wheel as round. Eyes are rounded with a dark circle in the middle. It is this left-brain ability however, that sometimes limits our creative thinking. Turn something upside down and your right brain will come into play. The left-brain doesn't do upside down because it does not recognize the symbols. What each of these exercises teaches us is that our memory isn't perfect. Before you can sculpt a replica of something, you first need to know what it really looks like. Sketching exercises will teach you to recognize details normally overlooked. With practice, you can learn to be more observant. Soon your eyes will begin to see the details, and your brain will remember them. Any object can be a helpful learning tool. Keep a pencil and paper handy. When you have a few minutes, sketch something close to you, a cup, a book, your hand, or maybe just one finger. The idea is to meticulously study the size and shape of the object, noting every individual detail. Does the light hit it from the side or from above? Where is the shadow? As you gain more experience you'll find yourself noticing these things automatically and will incorporate them into your work.

Following are some exercises you can do to improve your powers of observation.

Observe Family:

An easy way to strengthen your powers of observation is to spend some time studying your immediate family. Observe which features they share and make a simple chart. As you add members of your extended family, you can refer to your chart and quickly note if there are dominate traits in each generation or if they skip a generation. In my family, a dimple in the chin is a shared trait. Your parents or grandparents are all good sources of study material. You can make copies of old photos, enlarge them on a computer, and study the features to see what changes the years have made. Most photo programs have the ability to crop just a portion of the photo, which allows you to select individual features to compare.

We all have photos of our children. Pull out those baby pictures, as well as some a few years older. If they are grown, you most likely have an entire lineup from birth to an adult. What similarities do you see that are consistent throughout the years? Is there a particular shape to the eyebrows? Do they have a distinctive nose or even a crooked smile?

Observe Others:

The next time you are at the mall, find a seat and rest for a few minutes. Observe the people who walk by. I always find myself analyzing the people I see, who are they and why did they come to the mall today? Does a child look just like the parent? Why? Is it the overall shape of the face? Are the features alike or maybe their coloring? Try to determine precisely what the similarity is. In today's world, many people are wary of strangers. If you would like a closer look or maybe a picture of the parent and child, please ask the parent first. Most people are cooperative if they know your name and why you are interested in them. We all love to show off our children. It helps to carry business cards that identify you and your specialty. You can purchase packages of attractive business cards and postcards that are designed to be used on a computer. You simply add your information on the template provided and then print them out on the decorative papers.

Any place where people gather can be a chance to practice intelligent observation. In addition to observing faces, this is a good opportunity to observe other details. What type of hairstyles are teenagers wearing? Is it different from the hairstyles on older individuals of the same sex? Does long hair follow the head shape and how is it different from a short hairstyle? Is there a particular trend in clothing that everyone is wearing? How many men have facial hair? The ability to store these details in your brain and retrieve them from your memory is invaluable to an artist. Outdoor activities are especially good to observe people. In a more casual, relaxed setting, initiating a conversation is easier. Another good place to observe people is in church or another place where they wear a different type of clothing. How does it differ? How do they sit and how does their posture affect the way their clothing drapes? "People watching" can be a lot of fun and will go a long way towards improving your ability to recognize important characteristics.

Picture File:

If you haven't already started, begin a file of reference pictures, preferably close-ups of features. Pictures will not give you the 3-dimensional reference you get with a model but they will give you a variety of features to study. Fashion magazines are a good source of female faces of different races and frequently feature male models in the layouts. The eyes on fashion models are beautiful and very expressive. The close-up shots are perfect for seeing the shape and details of the eye. You will also find a wonderful selection of noses and differently shaped nostrils. Fashion models are normally very young so their lips are full and well-shaped. You can get an idea of how the lips stretch over the teeth to accommodate a smile. When teeth are visible, count the number of teeth that show in different poses. Practice drawing teeth. They are not picket-fence style; each one has its own shape, usually identical to the same tooth on the opposite side. You can also find close-up shots of men, women, and children in the hair design books at hair salons.

Publications like *Mature Living* and *AARP* are good for pictures of older adults. Do you assume they are older because you know it's a magazine for older people or are there differences that your brain associates with aging? Study the features. Exactly which changes do you see that indicates age to you? Are there lines or wrinkles? Folds of skin where the muscles have lost tone and become slack? Is the flesh along the jaw line soft and droopy? Is there excess skin on the neck? This is often called a turkey wattle as turkeys have a similar pouch of skin at the front of the throat.

Newspapers:

The Sunday newspaper has a section on weddings and engagements and there are usually pictures of couples celebrating their 50th Wedding Anniversary. Often there is a picture taken on their wedding day, alongside a recent one. Sometimes, it is quite surprising. They have aged, maybe gained weight or their hair is white, but it is clearly the same person. The shape of their face, their eyes, and their smile always stay the same. Maybe you have similar "before and after" pictures in your own family.

We are all familiar with the movie star, Humphrey Bogart. There is a biography that came out a few years ago, *Bogi: A Celebration of the Life and Films of Humphrey Bogart* (Schickel 2006). It's an excellent collection of pictures from his childhood to his death at age 57. As you turn the pages, you can see the changes in his face as he ages. This is a wonderful glimpse into the study of how features change, as we grow older. You can see where the expression lines began to show and which features become more pronounced over the years. The book should be available at your local library. It is an enjoyable book as well as being a good visual reference when you begin Part 8, Expression Lines and Part 9, The Aging Process.

Part Two

Ethnic Differences

Ethnic Differences

Eth·nic (eth-nik) 1. pertaining to or characteristic of a people, esp. a group (ethnic group) sharing a common and distinctive culture, religion, language, or the like.   Random House Dictionary, © Random House, Inc. 2010

*H*ave you ever wondered why we don't all look alike? After all, everyone has the same features in the same amounts. Two eyes, two ears, one nose, and one mouth...what makes one individual look different from the next? As you work through this book, you will come to realize the recognizable surface of the face is the sum total of the shape of the skull, muscles, and tissue and skin. Put on your Superman cape and use your x-ray vision to look beneath the skin - past the fat and under the muscles until you can envision the bony skull.

Before we get too far into the discussion of Ethnic Differences, I want to stress that the material provided in this book is a guide for artists – not a documentary. The skull used in the demonstrations in this book is a cast of a skull that was analyzed by an Osteologist, and classified based on current anthropological data. A portion of this Osteological Evaluation is included in the Glossary. The information and materials provided here are based on my personal research with individuals as well as published, scientific research. It isn't meant to cause offense, infringe on anyone's personal beliefs or be a debate on the reality of race. The question of race is controversial and ambiguous. In fact, the term itself is controversial and ambiguous. When referring to the races today, more commonly used terms are European-derived, African-derived and Asian-derived - or simply a person's ancestry. However, science currently recognizes three major races: Caucasoid, Negroid and Mongoloid, and some will add a fourth, Australoid (Aborigines).

The term Natural Drift, is used to describe the migration of peoples from region to region. It isn't clear who used the term originally or a precise reason for the migrations, but researchers believe it was often to find a more plentiful food supply or a more hospitable climate. Over many hundreds of years, this resulted in the blending of their origins. The different environments they faced further contributed to a variety of appearances within each group.

The temperature in some deserts near the equator often surpasses that of Death Valley. The skin produced more melanin as protection against the intense heat but some type of shelter was still necessary against the sun. They had to devise dwellings with the resources available. As with shelters, early humans had to adapt to the available food supply. The lack of water made it harder for humans and animals to exist. Without sufficient water, crops were not an option.

The Antarctica is the coldest recorded place on earth with Siberia, in Russia, holding the title of the coldest inhabitable place. People living in the extreme cold had to adapt to freezing temperatures. The occurrence of the epicanthic fold is believed to be an evolutionary defense against both the extreme cold as well as the extreme light that occurs in the Eurasian arctic and far north. The ice and blowing snow were a constant threat to life. Without the proper protection, an individual could die within minutes. They faced a constant search for food, and the hardships of obtaining clothing and shelter.

Although these were the extremes, history books document their many other difficulties. Some groups developed a nomadic lifestyle for survival. For others, it may have been to provide a better way of life for their families.

No one can be sure exactly how or when the earliest humans spread across the world, although the Out of Africa theory is probably still the most popular. With the emergence of DNA, scientists are discovering more about the migrations of early humans. A team of scientists from the NIOZ Royal Netherlands Institute for Sea Research and the University of Bremen (Germany) has determined that a major change in the climate of the Sahara and Sahel region of North Africa facilitated early human migrations from the African continent.

Climatic changes, oceanic changes, vegetation changes; no matter which theory you believe to be true it is a fascinating subject to study.

When I first became interested in forensic anthropology, I discovered the work of Forensic Anthropologist George Gill. Dr. Gill is recognized as an expert in skeletal biology. He has said that he is one of those very few physical anthropologists who actually does research on the particular traits used today in forensic racial identification or "assessing ancestry" as it is generally termed today. In the late 1980's, Dr. Gill tested, supported, and developed, '**craniofacial anthropometric**' means of estimating the racial origins of skeletal remains. He found that the employment of multiple criteria could yield very high rates of accuracy.

Craniofacial anthropometrics is the study of human body measurements, relating to the cranium and the face.

Anthropologists often deal with questions about race and/or the reality of race. As you can imagine they come down on both sides of the question and make valid observations based on their findings. I have always been a history buff and I find the books written by anthropologists very interesting.

Historical studies consistently show that each race has skeletal differences that serve to distinguish one from the other. In 2000 Dr. Gill served on a panel, along with five others who debated the reality of race.

> Dr. Gill writes, "*…the bony traits of the nose, mouth, femur, and cranium are just as revealing to a good Osteologist as skin color, hair form, nose form, and lips to the perceptive observer of living humanity. I have been able to prove to myself over the years, in actual legal cases, that I am more accurate at assessing race from skeletal remains than from looking at living people standing before me. So those of us in forensic anthropology know that the skeleton reflects race, whether 'real' or not, just as well if not better than superficial soft tissue does. The idea that race is 'only skin deep' is simply not true, as any experienced forensic anthropologist will affirm.*"

Does Race Exist? A proponent's perspective (Gill 2000 Nova Online)

Anthropologist C. Loring Brace, who took the opposing side on the panel, stated that the human inhabitants of the Western Hemisphere largely derive from three very separate regions of the world – Northeast Asia, Northwest Europe, and Western Africa. He said there is no biological entity that warrants the term race. There are features "…that we can easily identify as characteristic of the areas from which they come." He goes on to add that they would have to have resided in those places for a couple of hundred thousand years before their regional patterns become established.

As you can see, there is much more to this complicated subject than we could possibly cover in this book, or even several books. The purpose of bringing race into the discussion of observation, however, is to help you become aware of and utilize the known differences to your advantage as an artist.

According to the Frankfort Agreement of 1882, skulls were divided into three shapes, originally using the Cephalic Index.

- Dolichocephalic – A long, narrow head shape
- Mesocephalic – A medium head shape
- Brachycephalic - A broad head shape

Today we use simpler terms to describe the head shape. Narrow, Medium and Broad. When working with skulls it's necessary to place the skull in a very specific, level position to obtain valid comparisons. Known as the Frankfort Horizontal Plane, it is an imaginary line that passes through the lowest point of the Orbital Cavity and the upper edge of the Auditory Meatus; the opening to the ear canal. Anthropologists use 28 skeletal measurements as guidelines in assigning racial affinity. There are a few characteristics though that can be visible to the naked eye. Study these images of male and female skulls (Figures 2-1 and 2-2). Notice the differences in each of the three ethnic groups: Caucasoid, Negroid, and Mongoloid. Compare the shape and size of the Orbital Cavity (eyes), the Nasal Cavity (nose), and the shape and width of the Zygomatic Bones (cheekbones). Note that the width and shape of the Mandible (jawbone) is different between males and females, as well as each ethnic group.

Figures 2-1 through 2-12 list some of the more visible differences.

Caucasoid Skulls (European-derived)

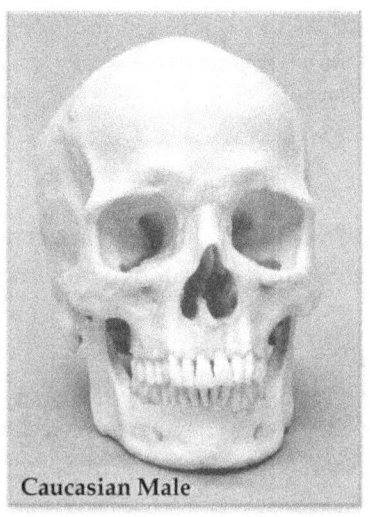

Caucasian Male

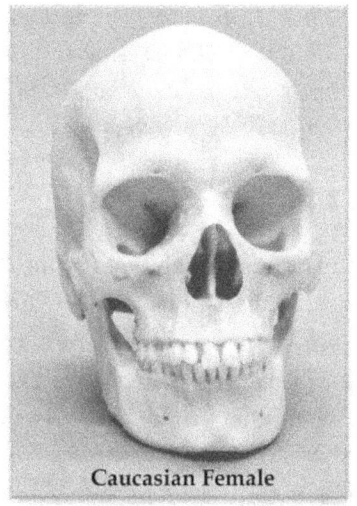

Caucasian Female

African Male (Negroid)

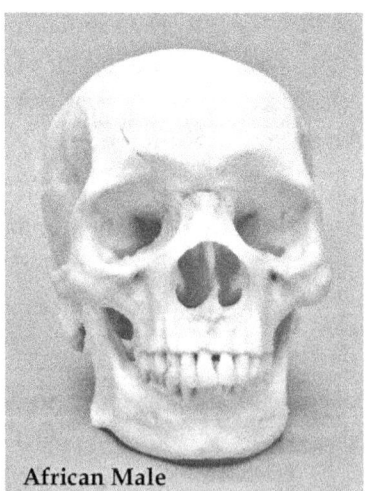

African Male

Figure 2-1

14

Negroid Skulls (African-derived)

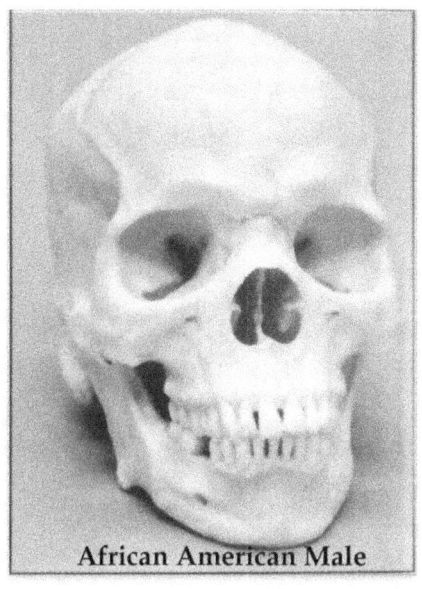

African American Male

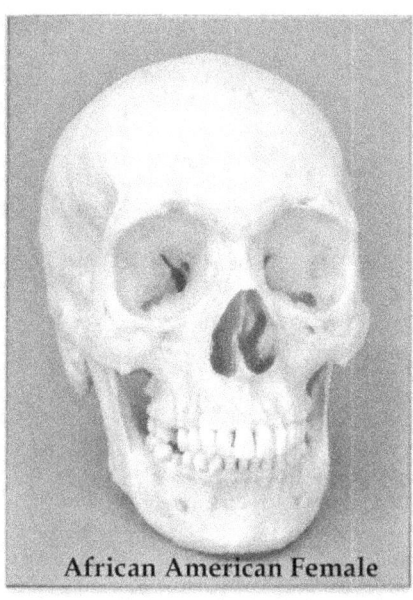

African American Female

Mongoloid Skulls (Asian-derived)

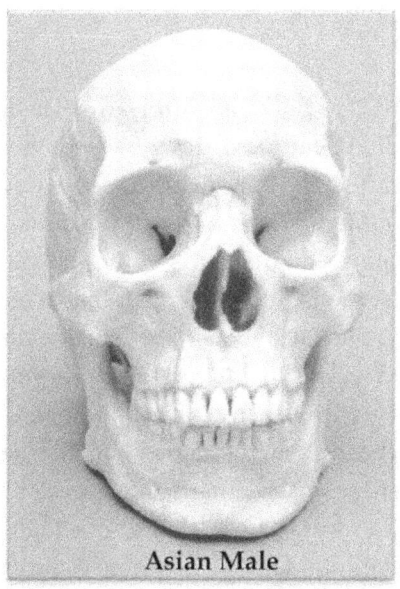

Asian Male

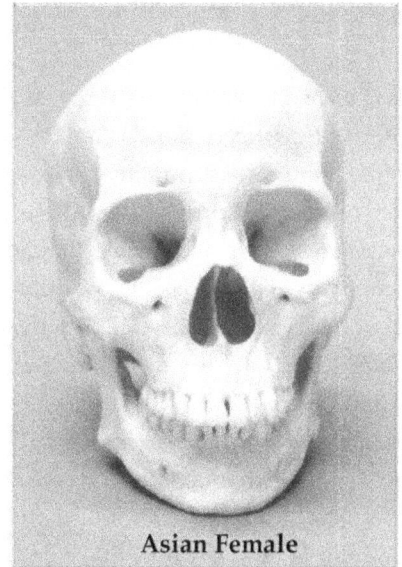

Asian Female

Figure 2-2

Caucasoid – European derived

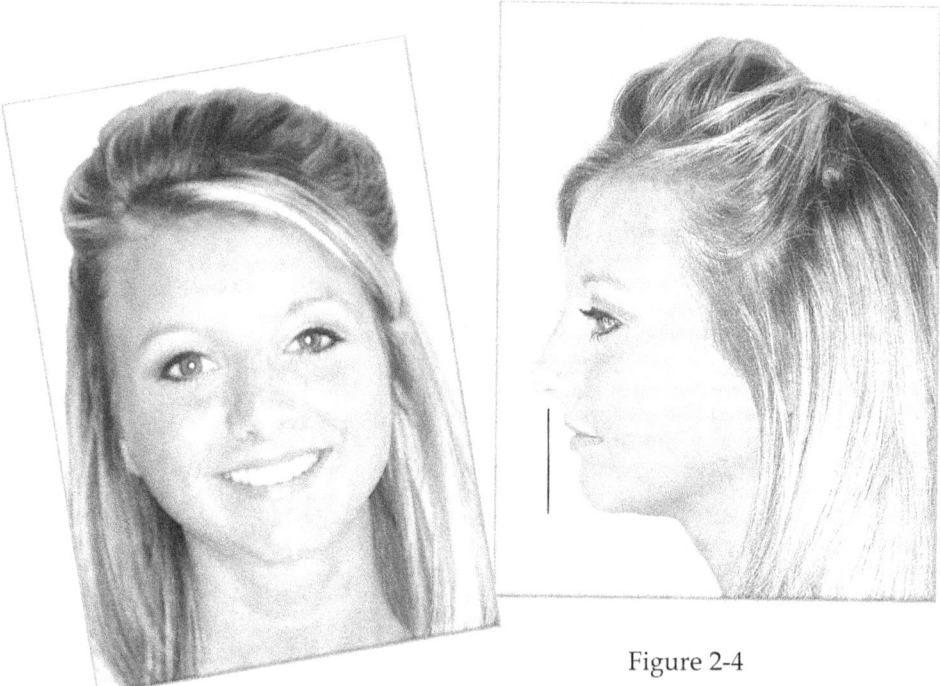

Figure 2-4

Figure 2-3

The Caucasoid race covers the groups generally known as Europeans. The term Caucasoid, is used most often in the United States, to describe people who originally migrated from the region of Caucasus. The build will vary between the taller Northern Europeans and the shorter Mediterranean's to the south. The Caucasian skull is ovoid (egg-shaped) and the individual parts of the skull are in harmony with none being unduly prominent (Figure 2-3). The shape of the orbital cavity is angular and slightly sloping. The facial bones are Orthognathous (straight up and down) and a pencil held vertically under the nose will be straight (Figure 2-4). The nose is long and narrow with tear shaped openings; and may be straight or hooked. The forehead is high; the Zygomatic bones (cheekbones) are narrow and receding. The chin is prominent, especially in males. The skull measured top to bottom and front to back, will be of equal size. Skin color is light to olive. Eye color can be light to dark. Hair color can vary and be straight or wavy. The characteristics tend to follow geographic boundaries.

Negroid – African derived

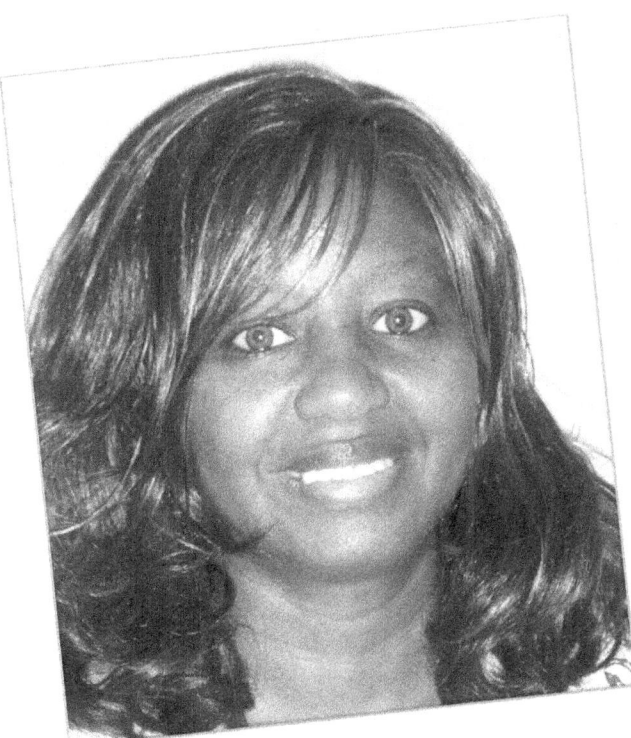

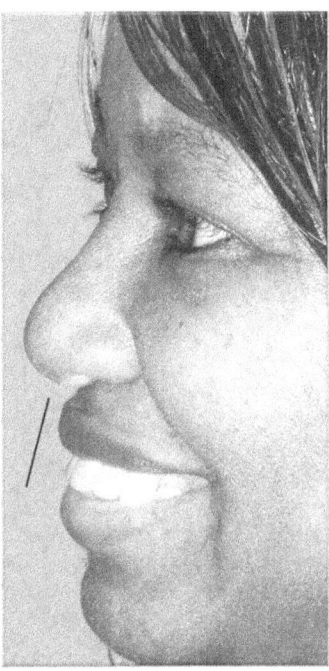

Figure 2-6

Figure 2-5

The Negroid race originally referred to the African Negro. They have a medium build though there can be a wide variation in stature and coloring between the northern and southern regions. In the United States today, we most often use the term African-American. The skull is rather flat across the top. The forehead may be flat and receding or rounded and rise straight up from the brows. The eyes are rounder and set further apart. The nose is broad and flat, resulting in nostrils that are wider and shorter (Figure 2-5). The Zygomatic bones are broad, larger than the Caucasoid, but still receding. The lips are wider in height and fully everted (turned out).The lower jaw is large and strong, especially in males. The chin is smaller and rounded. Skin color ranges from light to dark brown to almost black. The eyes are dark; the hair is dark and a course texture. One of the most prominent Negroid features is **Prognathism**, the projection of the lower portion of the face. A pencil held vertically under the nose will project outward (Figure 2-6).

Mongoloid – Asian derived

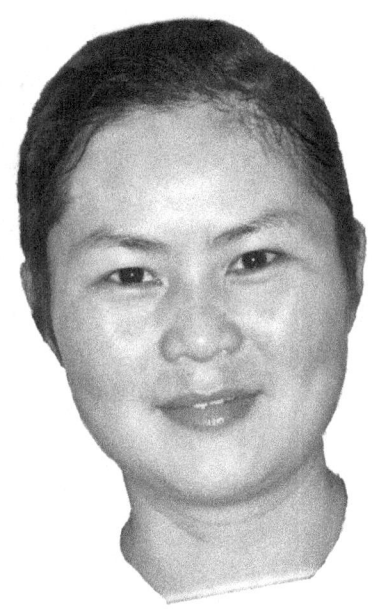

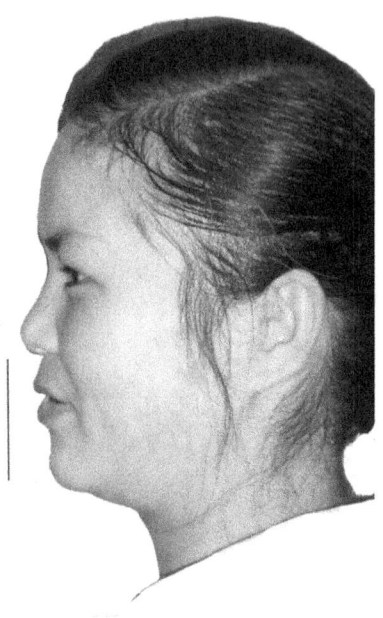

Figure 2-8

Figure 2-7

The Mongoloid race covers most of the Asian populations. Some areas produce tall individuals though most will have a smaller stature and shorter legs. The skull is broad (brachycephalic), and rounded across the dome. It will usually measure slightly shorter front to back, than top to bottom. The face is round (Figure 2-7), and the facial bones are flatter resulting in the entire profile being flatter. A pencil held vertically under the nose will be straight Figure 2-8). The forehead is high with a small brow ridge. The cheek area is wider with projecting Zygomatic bones (cheekbones). The nose is flatter than the Caucasoid and of medium width. The lips fall somewhat between the Caucasoid and the Negroid. The chin is slightly projecting. Straight, black hair is the norm. The skin usually has a yellow-brown tinge. The eyes are dark and may be straight or have a distinct slant, exhibiting the **Epicanthic Fold**. The Epicanthic Fold refers to the vertical fold of skin covering the Inner Canthus, the inner corner of the eye. The Epicanthic Fold is also called the Epicanthus Fold.

In addition to Asians, the Mongoloid race includes Eskimos and American Indians. They typically have quite round faces, the flatter profile, and a less projecting brow bone. They may also exhibit the Epicanthic Fold. Within groups however, there will be individual characteristics. Our first model is Apache Indian. The Apache Tribe consists of six sub-tribes each from a different geographical region. He shows a slight Epicanthic Fold, and a round face (Figure 2-9). The flatter profile and projecting Zygomatic Bones (cheekbones) are typical of the Mongoloid race (Figure 2-10). Dark eyes, flat nose, rounded chin and straight, black hair are the norm. They have little facial or body hair. Their skin color ranges from yellow-brown to reddish brown.

Apache Indian – Asian derived

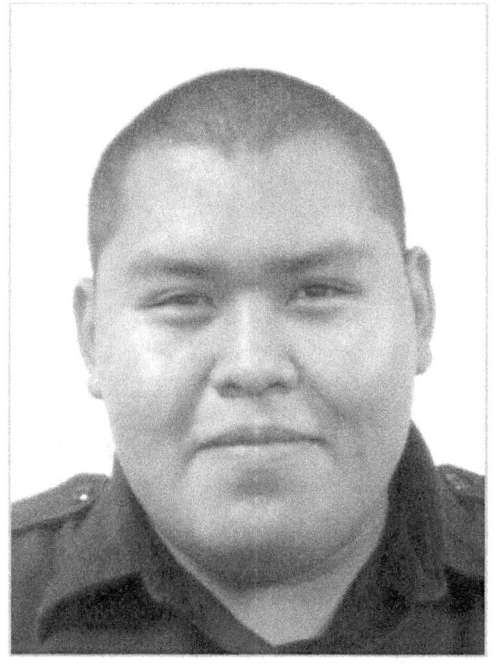

Figure 2-9

Figure 2-10

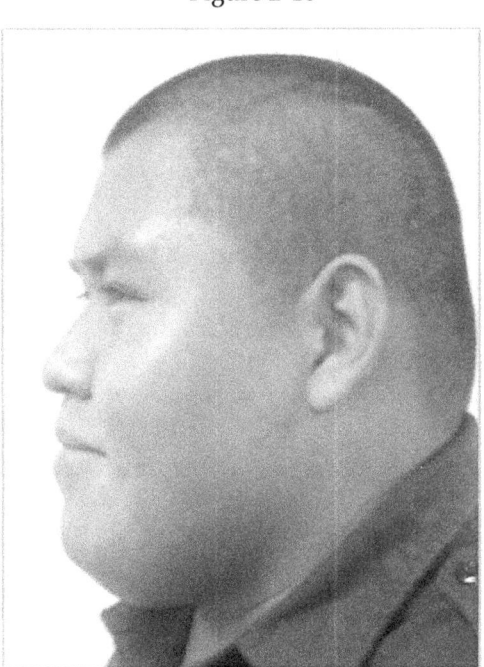

Our second model is Laotian, from Laos in Southern Asia. He exhibits the typical Mongoloid features, the rounded skull, a broad, round face with a flat nose, and a rounded chin. He has a slight epicanthic fold though it is harder to see with his glasses (Figure 2-11). He has a flatter profile (Figure 2-12) and the Zygomatic bones (cheekbones) are still projecting though less so than the previous model.

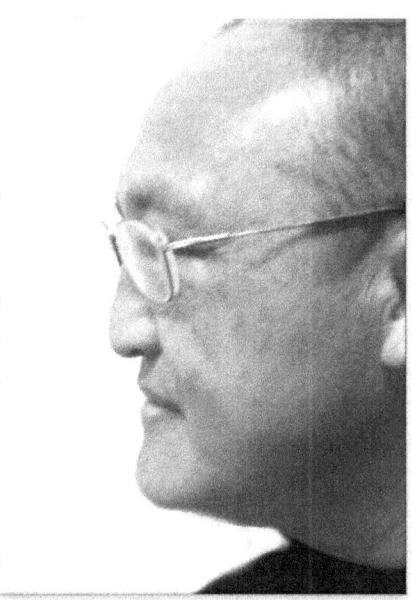

Figure 2-12

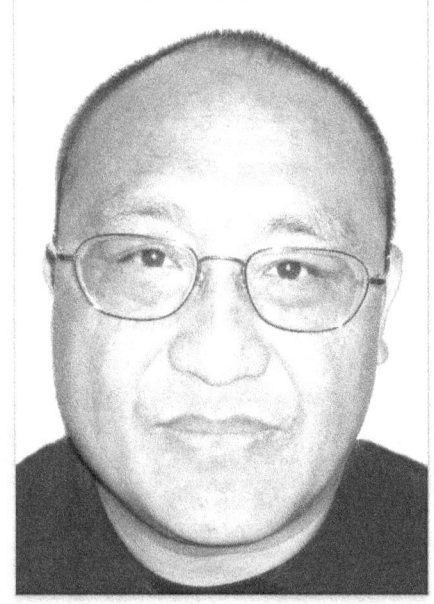

Figure 2-11

If you plan to sculpt an individual of a race other than your own, it's important to find a model so you can study individual details. We are so accustomed to what we see in the mirror and around us; it's hard for us to detect the individual differences in other races. If possible, spend some time with the person before you begin. If nothing else, search for a variety of photographs that portray that race. Your sculpting will be more professional and everyone will appreciate the correct details.

Zygomatic bones are said to be projecting or receding based on the lower portion of the front of the zygomatic bone (cheekbone). A receding cheekbone projects backwards. A projecting zygomatic bone actually drops straight down. It is said to be projecting in Mongoloids, in relation to the receding zygomatic bones of Caucasians and Negroids.

All of the characteristics we've mentioned in this section are also seen in children (Figure 2-13).

Figure 2-13

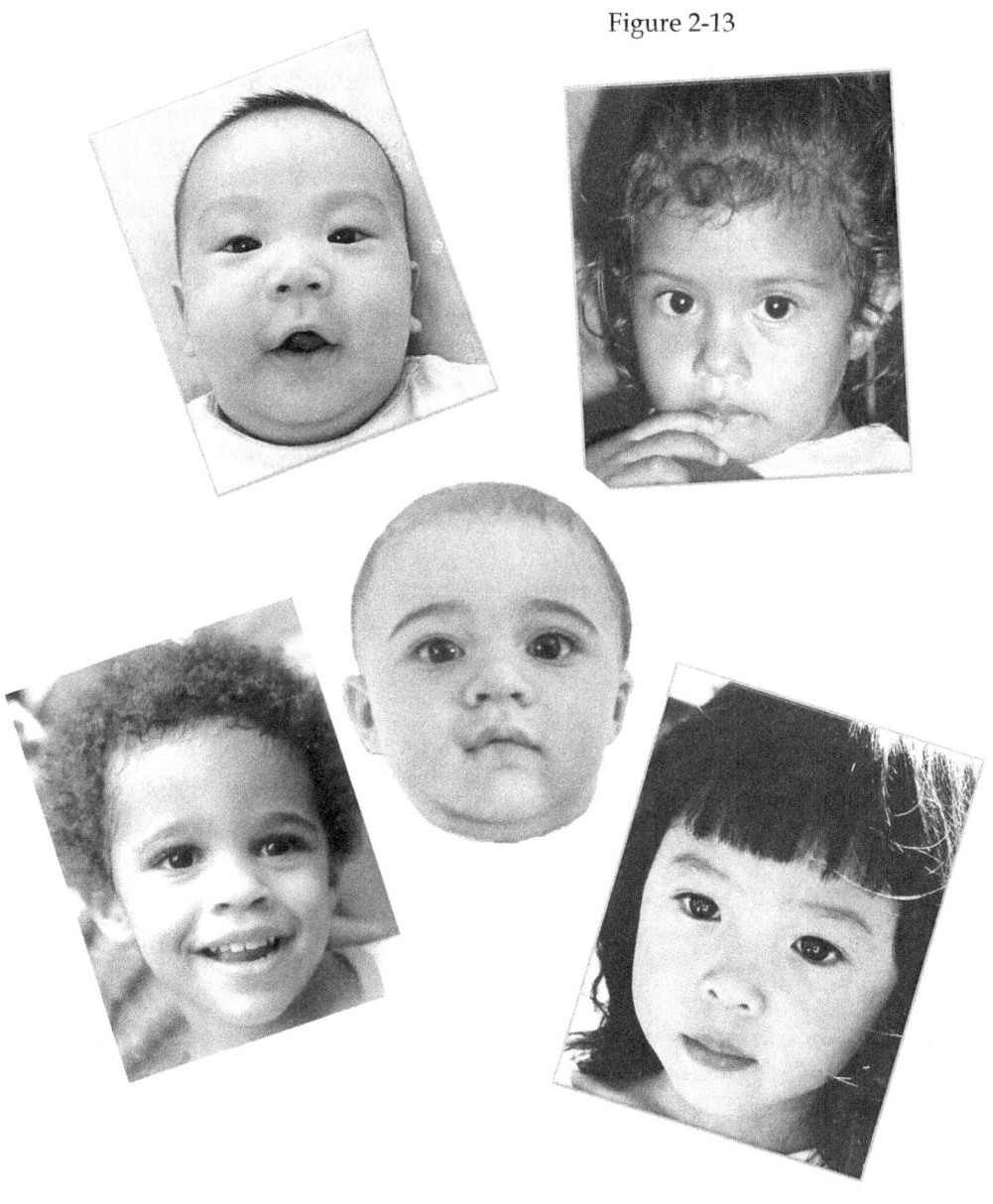

How an Anthropologist Determines Race, Gender, and Age

It's important to note right at the beginning that a Forensic Anthropologist would never make a judgment of race, gender or age based on a single indicator. The conclusion is always based on all the available information. Not only the bones, but also any other items found with the skeleton and/or other information law enforcement might determine from the scene.

If you have studied the characteristics of the three major races in this chapter, you know the skull has identifiers as to race, sex, and age. There are skeletal differences between the races, between male and female, as well as, between individuals of a given race. Overall, a male skull will be larger and stronger than a female. The extra muscle strength in men will be apparent in the strength of their muscle attachments to the bone; those areas on the skull are remarkably rougher. The eyebrow ridge is larger, projecting, and very well defined. This gives the eyes a deep-set look, and the forehead tends to slant backwards. The Mandible (lower jawbone) in the male is larger than that of a female therefore increasing the width and size of the lower face. The chin is square, more pronounced and the angle of the Mandible at the Ramus (the vertical portion of bone at the back of the mandible) will be sharper. This gives the male skull a square appearance.

The female skull is generally smaller overall and has a more refined appearance. The eyebrow ridge is sharper though less projecting. The angle of the Mandible is subtle, not as defined and the chin of a female appears more rounded. As in life, the male is larger, stronger, and more angular than females, who are generally smaller, have less muscular strength, and project a softer appearance.

If you want your men to look like men and your women to look like women, it is important to be aware of these unique differences and maintain the distinctions in your work.

The skull helps establish racial affinity. In addition, the size and shape are taken into consideration when determining the gender.

The hip and the pelvis are two distinct, but interrelated parts of the body that form the base of the torso. The pelvis provides a foundation for the movement of the back and legs, and permits the weight of the entire upper body to be evenly distributed to the legs, which are connected to the pelvis through the hip joints. The Pelvis, located at the base of the spine, is also the primary determiner of gender. Like the skull, the pelvis of a female will appear more delicate. It is also wider and shallower than the male. The angle of the Pubic Arch is often used as a visual determiner of gender. The difference in the size and shape between the male and female pelvis can be seen in these pictures.

Forensic Anthropologist Dr. Ted Rathbun, professor emeritus of anthropology at the University of South Carolina, mentions a quick rule of thumb he found very reliable. If the …angle is about the same as between the outstretched thumb and index finger, it is most likely a female pelvis. If it's closer to the angle between the spread index and middle finger, it is a male pelvis.

The **Pubic Arch** is shown in these illustrations from Gray's Anatomy 1918. The female pelvis (Figure 2-14), and the male pelvis (Figure 2-15).

Figure 2-14 **Female Pelvis**   Figure 2-15 **Male Pelvis**

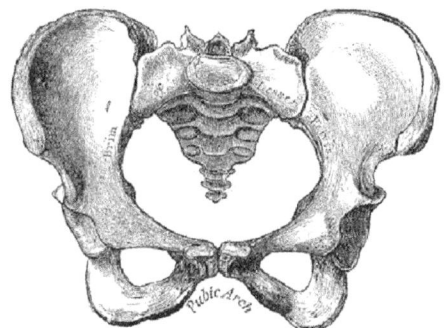   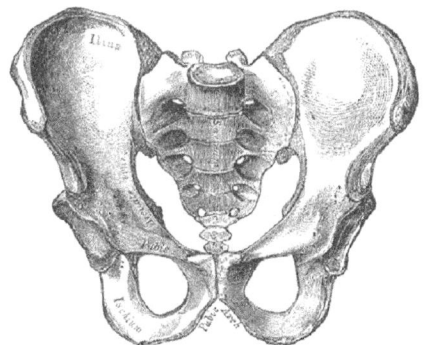

Wide Angle of the Female   **Sharp Angle of the Male**

Several different guidelines are used to establish age. Stature is determined by measuring the Arm Bones, Leg Bones, and the Metatarsals, (the bones in the ball of the foot). Anthropologists will also consider the stages of growth, indications of disease and/or injuries present. Age in a younger person is determined by checking which stages of growth have occurred. Teeth erupt on a regular timetable and the growth stage of the jaw is significant. The closing of the Sutures in the skull and the joining of the bones also occur in individuals about the same time. Once a person reaches the age of 35 to 40 years old, and growth is finished, the anthropologist will need to reply on other indicators. For instance, arthritic changes might indicate an older individual.

When teeth are present and dental charts are available, they may be used to make a positive identification. Teeth are the hardest substance in the body. Bones can succumb to age, deterioration, or animal destruction. Teeth, however, are susceptible only to the natural forces of tooth decay. Teeth do not decompose or change and according to the American Dental Association, external forces such as fires or floods cannot destroy them.

Forensic Anthropologists, working with law enforcement, use all available information to determine an individual's identity – as well as to rule out other individuals. They will never makes a determination of race, gender or age based on just one or two details, but will examine all available bones, teeth, and any additional evidence that law enforcement may be able to provide.

Part Three

Bone Structure of the Skull

Bone Structure of the Skull

*T*o achieve the best results from the material presented in this book, it's important to become familiar with the location of the bones and the structure of the skull identified in this section.

What country would you most like to visit? For me, it would be Italy. The art, the sculpture, and the food all call to me like the siren's song of Greek Mythology. If you won an all-expense paid trip to the country of your dreams, you'd want to do everything you could to make the most of your experience. You might buy a book to learn about the country and a bilingual dictionary to figure out the signs. Tourist's guidebooks have a section of commonly asked questions and phrases. There will be a phrase in your native language then the same phrase in the language of the country you plan to visit. I speak some Spanish and a little French, but no Italian. If I were lucky enough to win a trip to Italy, I would definitely want to learn as much as I could so that when I stepped off the plane I'd be ready to start discovering Italy.

This is the way it is with the bones in the skull. The words sound like a foreign language the first time you read them. They are confusing tongue twisters that make no sense at all. However, once you understand how the structure of the skull affects our outer appearance, you will be in a better position to sculpt realistic faces. As you study and practice, one day it will all fall into place for you. You'll pick up a pencil or a handful of clay and your fingers will immediately know where to begin.

For an artist, knowing what's on the inside will naturally lead to the correct form on the outside.

When my boys were young, we lived in California, which had been famous for its citrus production for many years. As competition increased, Sunkist growers began putting a trademark sticker on each orange they sold. They ran a television commercial showing a monster jumping out of a "non-Sunkist" orange with the tag line …"if it doesn't say Sunkist on the outside, you don't know what's on the inside". For years, my boys would not eat an orange that didn't have a Sunkist sticker. They were always quick to remind me that if it doesn't say Sunkist on the outside, you don't know what's on the inside.

If you've ever held an infant, you were careful to protect the head. Specifically, the soft spot on the top of the head, the Anterior Fontelle. The "soft spot" is actually strong, fibrous cartilage that holds together the two Parietal bones and the Occipital bone on the infant's skull.

One reason for the cartilage (called Sutures), is to allow the bones to move during the birth process, which sometimes gives an infant a lopsided head at birth. Another reason is so the skull can accommodate the rapidly growing brain. This bit of leeway also allows enough movement to avoid fractures in the skull as the baby begins to get around.

About the time a child is walking well (usually by 18 months), the sutures on the top of the head close. By about age 25, all the sutures on the skull will have completely closed. As individuals continue to age, the sutures ossify and change soft tissue (such as cartilage) into bone, and may no longer be visible on a skull.

The skull has two parts: the **Cranium** (the upper portion that holds the brain) and the **Mandible** (the lower portion that forms the jaw). Similar to a jigsaw puzzle, the sutures form interlocking "seams" that run across the top, back and sides of the skull to hold the bones of the Cranium in place. The four major sutures on the skull are the **Coronal**, the **Sagittal,** the **Squamosal** and the **Lamboid.**

Figure 3-1 shows the **Sagittal Suture**, which runs front to back between the **Coronal Suture** and the **Lamboid Suture** and connects the two Parietal Bones.

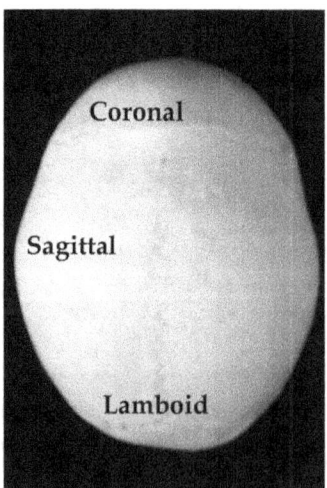

Figure 3-1

In this view, you see the **Coronal Suture** horizontally across the top of the skull (Figure 3-2).

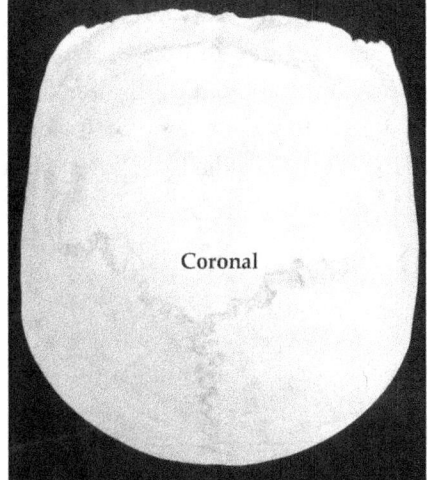

Figure 3-2

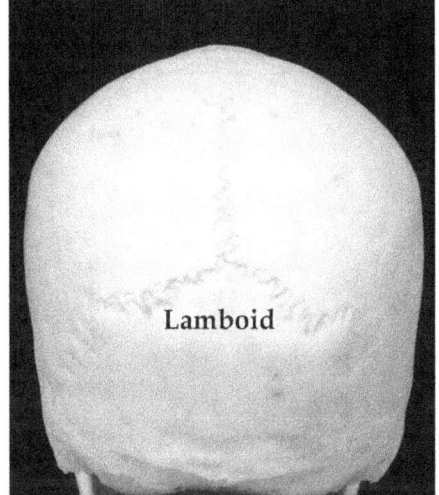

Figure 3-3

The **Lamboid Suture** runs horizontally across the back of the skull (Figure 3-3).

The **Squasomal Sutures** (Figure 3-4), connect the Parietal bones to the Temporal Bones on both sides of the skull.

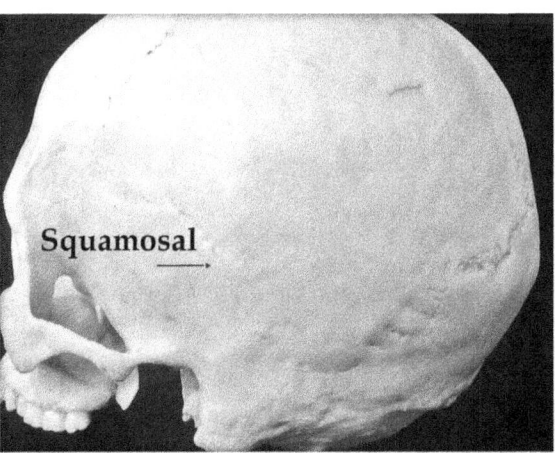

Figure 3-4

Figure 3-5 will help you locate the bones of the skull. The **Coronal Suture** joins the **Frontal Bone** and the **Parietal Bones**. The **Lamboid Suture** joins the **Parietal Bones** and the **Occipital Bone**. **The Squamosal Suture** joins the **Parietal Bones** to the **Temporal Bone** on both sides of the head. The **Sagittal Suture**, on the top of the skull, joins the two **Parietal Bones**.

Bones of the Skull - Profile

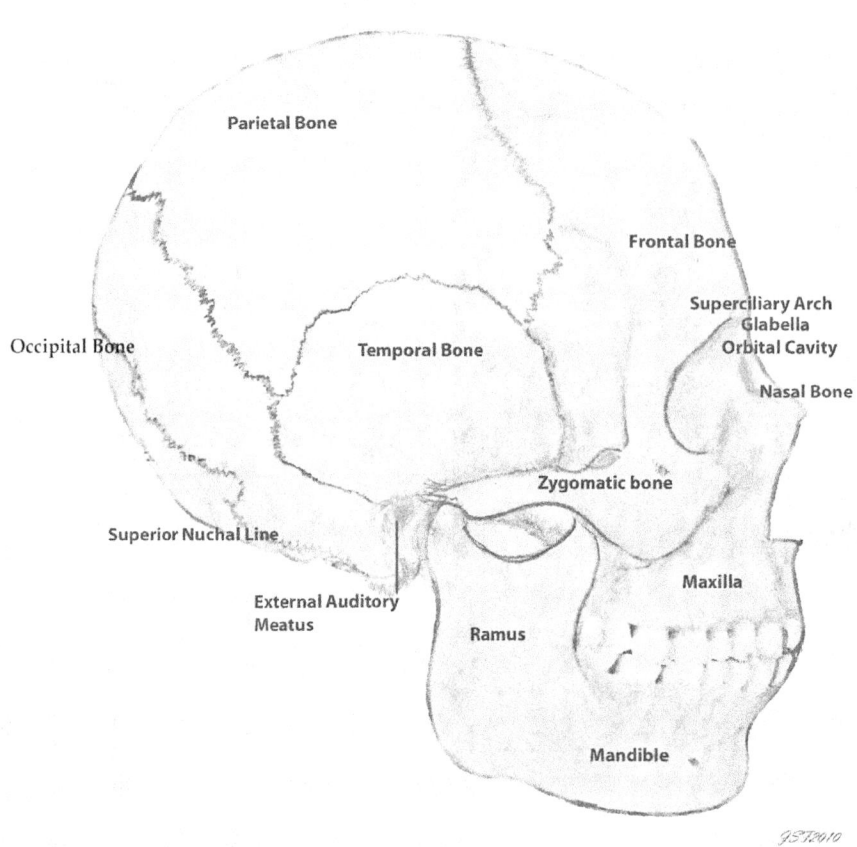

Figure 3-5

The bones of the cranium protect the brain and the facial bones provide the framework for the face. They protect and support the eyes, nose, mouth, and lips (Figure 3-6).

Facial Bones

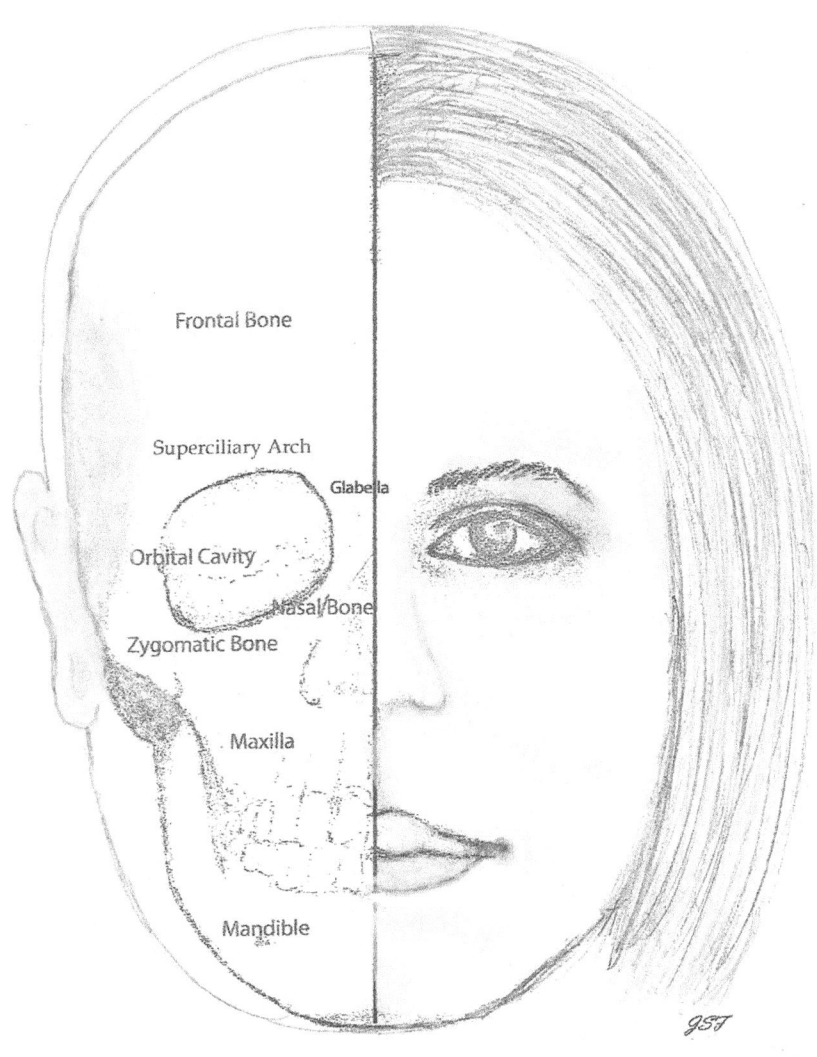

Figure 3-6

Locate the bones of the face on the drawing (Figure 3-6), then practice the following exercise to familiarize yourself with the structure of the face.

- Look in a mirror and visualize the major bones of the skull. Use your fingers to press around the **Orbital Cavity** (eye sockets). Press gently yet firm enough to feel the shape of the bone. Close your eyes and feel the roundness of the eyeball – it sits in the center of the orbital cavity. Continue moving your fingers out to the side of each eye and feel the slight depression in front of the **Temporal Bone** (temple area). There is also a depression at the outer end of the **Supraorbital Ridge** (another name for the brow bone; also called the **Superciliary Arch**). Trace your eyebrows to see how they follow the ridge. With your three middle fingers above each eyebrow, feel the shallow depression just above the ridge, and then slide them up the **Frontal Bone** (forehead) into the hairline. Feel how your forehead curves up and back. Use a mirror to check your profile to see the curve of the **Frontal Bone**.

- With your hair pulled back, have someone take a picture of you in profile, and check everything from a different angle. It will be easier to understand, once you have a visual of how the Frontal Bone rises from the brow ridge and continues to curve up to the top of the skull.

- At the top of the nasal bone, you can feel the angle of the **Glabella** change as it blends into the **Frontal Bone**. This is not a separate bone but the small area above the nasal bone and between the eyebrows. This is the transition from the nasal bone to the frontal bone. The easiest way to feel the angle is press two fingers above the nasal bone, right between the eyebrows. Move your fingers around and up and down until you feel the angle change. This might be easier to feel if you close your eyes and go by touch alone.

- The angle of the **Glabella** is more prominent in males, and is an important distinction when sculpting men. By contrast, the female has a softer angle that merges with the **Frontal Bone**. Along with a projecting brow bone, the angle of the **Glabella** is a major point in drawing or sculpting adult males.

- The **Nasal Bone** forms the bridge of the nose, and its angle determines the shape of your nose. Press firmly across the top and side areas of your nose to feel where the **Nasal Bone** ends and the cartilage begins. A smooth transition here will result in a straight nose. A bump on your nose may be the result of an uneven transition.

> **The Glabella is a small, but important angular area of bone that is above the nasal bone and below the frontal bone. The forehead does not rise straight up from the nose.**

- As you come down the sides of your nose, there is a depression below the bone and just above the nostrils. This is an important detail in sculpting realistic noses.

- Continue pressing from the bridge of the nose outward. The nasal bone spreads out in a tent-like manner to join the **Zygomatic Bone** along the lower edge of the **Orbital Cavity.** Feel along the **Zygomatic Bone** as it curves around to the ear to the **Temporal Bone**, creating the cheekbones and forming the **Zygomatic Arch.**

- Below the nose is the **Maxilla -** the upper jawbone that holds the upper teeth. The **Maxilla** drops down from the **Zygomatic Bone** and curves around under it. Place your fingers below your nose and press firmly against your teeth. Walk your fingers back on each side to feel the shape of the **Maxilla.** You can see the muscles pull the lips back, and around, this curve when you smile.

- The Mandible, the lower jawbone, holds the lower teeth and forms a horseshoe shape that curves from front to back under the Maxilla. At the back of the Mandible the bone angles upwards to form the Ramus. At the top of the Ramus is the Mandible Knob - a ball-like end that forms a hinge with the Temporal Bone. If you follow the angle of the Ramus up to just in front of the ear and open your mouth wide, you can feel the action as the lower jaw drops down and back.

The **Mandible** on a male is wider, stronger, and more projecting. The chin is also squarer on a male than a female. The acute angle of the **Ramus** gives the male skull a square appearance overall. In a female, the **Mandible** is smaller and more refined. The angle of the **Ramus** is softer, and the chin tends to be rounder.

This image of a male skull (Figure 3-7), shows the square, slightly flared angle where the **Ramus** begins. In contrast, the angle of the female **Mandible** (Figure 3-8) is rounded, and the entire look is softer.

The Mandible is the only completely detachable bone on the adult skull. As the cartilage deteriorates, the Mandible loosens. On skeletal remains, weather or animals may scatter the bones. The result is the mandible is often missing when skeletal remains are discovered.

The female skull is higher and rounded as opposed to the male, which is flatter. The male skull is deeper than a female, measured front to back, and the entire mandible is wider making the face broader.

Male Skull

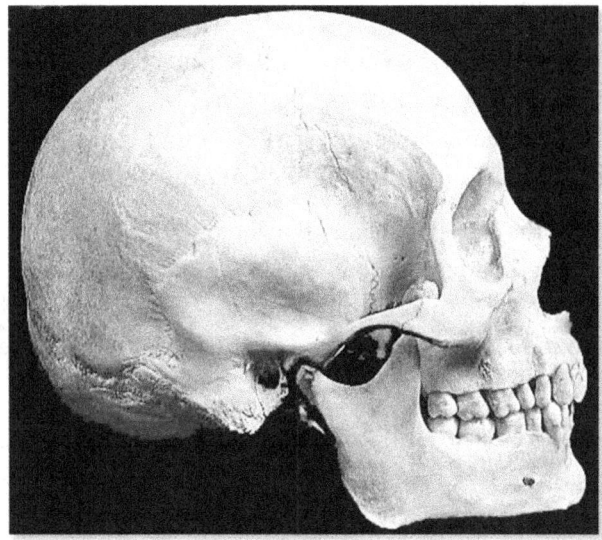

Figure 3-7

Female Mandible

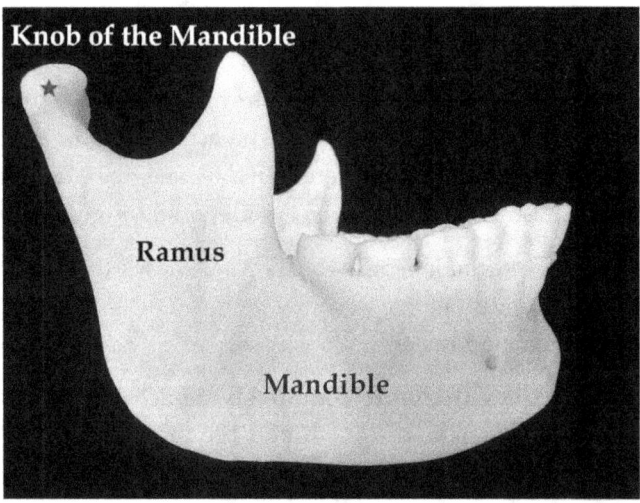

Figure 3-8

The knob at the very top of the **Ramus** is where the **Mandible** attaches to the skull, forming the Temporomandibular Joint (TMJ). This unique joint is what allows us to articulate the jaw, moving it up, down, forward and side-to-side.

The **Ramus** forms an upright angle at the back of the **Mandible.** At the top of the **Ramus**, the skull makes an impressive change of shape. The outward curve begins at the **Superior Nuchal Line** to form the rounded **Cranium** (Figure 3-9). This large, rounded portion is where the brain is located. A*rtists need to be aware of the size of the cranium. The skull is the same size measured front to back, as it is top to bottom.*

The **Superior Nuchal Line** refers to the ridge, or crest, where the large muscles connect the **Cranium** to the vertebral column. Cup the back of your neck and slide your hand up. You will feel this ridge on your own skull. The strong muscles attached here support the neck and balance the head on the body.

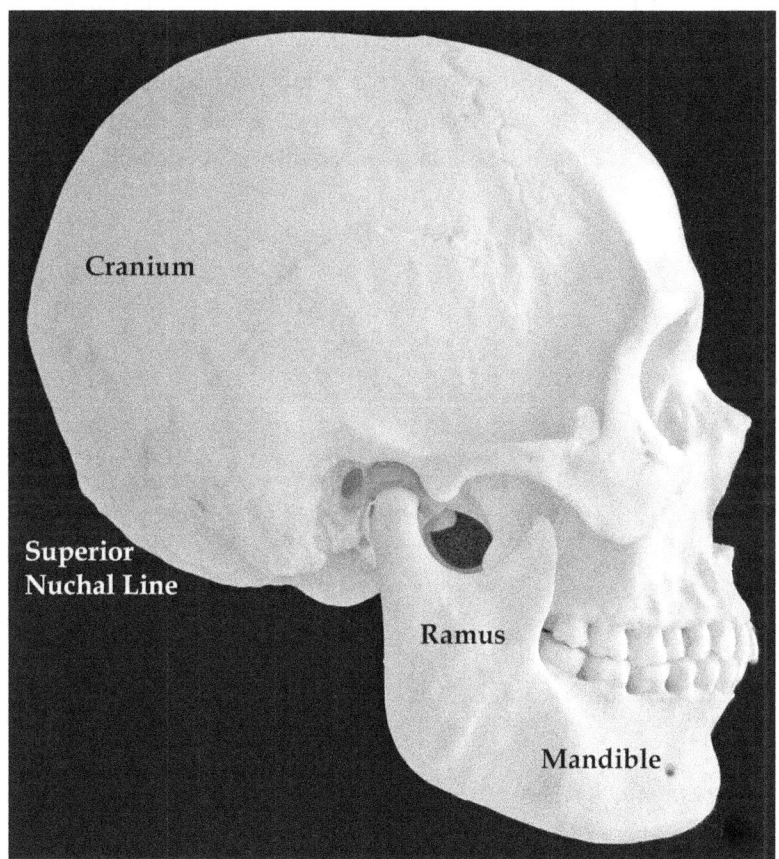

Figure 3-9

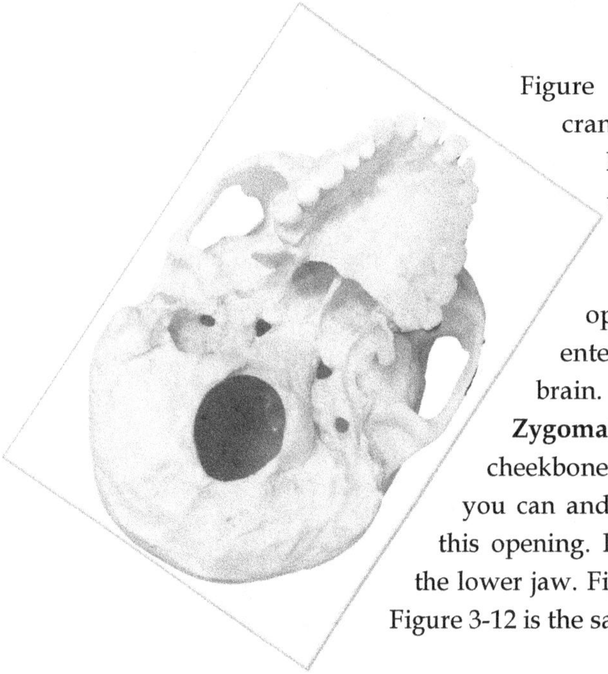

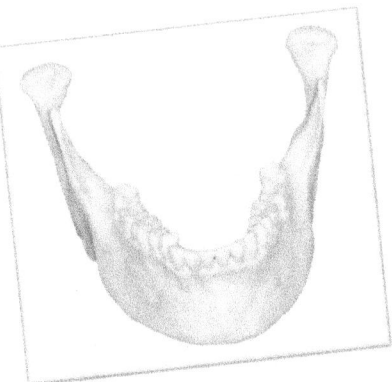

Figure 3-10 shows the underside of the cranium, minus **the mandible. You can see how the maxilla, the upper** jaw, holds the upper teeth and curves around in a horseshoe shape. The large hole in the cranium is the **Foramen Magnum.** This opening allows the spinal column to enter the skull where it attaches to the brain. On either side of the maxilla, the **Zygomatic Arches** widen out, forming the cheekbones. If you suck in your cheeks as hard as you can and follow the maxilla back, you can feel this opening. It's below your cheekbones and above the lower jaw. Figure 3-11 is the separate mandible and Figure 3-12 is the same skull with the mandible attached.

Figure 3-10

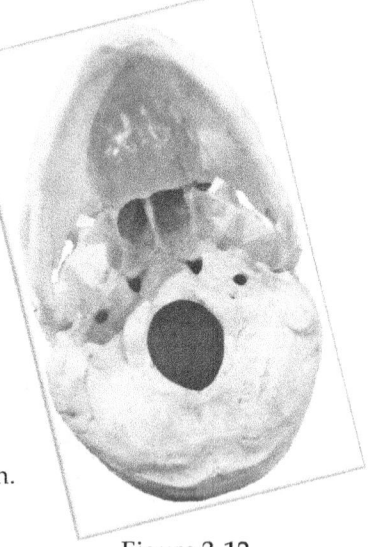

Figure 3-11 (above) is the Mandible, the lower jawbone, as it looks apart from the Cranium.

Figure 3-12

Part Four

Tissue Depth Charts

Tissue Depth Charts

The use of tissue depth measurements to reconstruct a human face isn't new. German anatomists were using tissue depth measurements as early as the late 1800's. Originally, the technique was used to recreate faces of famous persons. It was first used in the USA in 1926 for the facial reconstruction of a prehistoric human skull. Over time as the technique was improved, it spread into forensic science to assist with identification of the dead.

Dr. Stanley Rhine working with colleagues from the University of New Mexico used cadavers to obtain newer measurements. The results were published in 1980, revised in 1982 and 1984. The new charts showed average tissue depths for American Caucasians, American Negroids, Asian-Derived, and American Indians. An advantage of the new charts was that they were divided by race, gender, and different weights. Using male and female cadavers, they measured the depth of the tissues at 21 specific bony landmarks on the skull. The process used a calibrated needle inserted into soft tissue until it reached bone, and then the measurement was recorded. The number represented the total depth of the muscle, fat, tissue, and skin in one measurement.

Betty Pat. Gatliff was working as a Medical Illustrator in 1967 when forensic anthropologist Dr. Clyde Snow asked her assistance in preparing a facial reconstruction of a Native American male. She studied the information published by Dr. Wilton Krogman in his book, *The Human Skeleton in forensic Medicine* (1962), before attempting the reconstruction.

Working with Dr. Snow, Betty Pat. Gatliff later developed and refined a method of facial reconstruction, now called the American Method. This method uses vinyl markers, cut to precise lengths using the Tissue Depth Charts, then glued to the skull at the identical locations shown on the charts. The artist applies clay to the depth of the markers to develop a rough outline of the face. The success of this method relies on the information provided by an anthropologist and the artists' ability to read the skull correctly. The early success of this method led to law enforcement using facial reconstruction more often to identify skeletal remains. It was easier for officers to learn this method as they didn't need the extensive knowledge of anatomy required by other methods.

Between 1998 and 2000, Professor Mary Manhein, Louisiana State University, gathered newer measurements using ultrasound techniques. 551 children and 256 adult volunteers took part in the study. Most people believe that these ultrasound measurements are more precise as the difference in skin tension and gravity from living, breathing individuals is more reliable. The work done with children is definitely more precise. The charts on children include white and black American children. The differences in adults, however, did not vary substantially from previously published statistics. There are differences, but not substantial differences. The measurements for adults include male and female, both white and black plus five different ethnic groups. Mary Manhein is Director of the Forensic Anthropology and Computer Enhancement Services lab at Louisiana State University and the author of *The Bone Lady, Life as a Forensic Anthropologist* (2000). When I checked with Professor Manhein a couple of years ago, she said this data was still the most recent for children. At that time, however, they were working on two new projects. One project focused on Chinese American adults and the other on Native Canadians, adults and children. The study on Chinese American adults has been completed and will be published in the Journal of Forensic Sciences early in 2011.

The project on Canadian Aboriginal populations used the same ultra sound methods employed by Manhein et al. (2000). Dr. Tanya R. Peckmann, Saint Mary's University (Halifax, Canada) was the first author on this project and recently shared the following information.

Project background & methods:

To date, North American indigenous populations are under-represented in the forensic data. Presently, no data exist for facial tissue thickness in Canadian Aboriginal populations. This project utilized ultrasound technology to measure facial soft tissue depths in living Canadian Mi'kmaq children (Mi'kmaq are an Aboriginal group originating in the Canadian Maritime region, i.e. East Coast).

Researchers measured 19 points across the face (right side only) for 392 children aged three to eighteen years using the same ultrasound machine employed by Manhein et al.

Hiring Aboriginal students was a very important part of this research project. Their knowledge helped facilitate the research so that the dialogue exchange was culturally significant for both Aboriginal and non-Aboriginal individuals.

The necessity of this project arises from the increased violence experienced by Aboriginal peoples, especially children. Canadian Aboriginals are at a higher risk for being victims than the Canadian population in general. Aboriginal youth have the highest rate of suicide and family violence is more common in Aboriginal communities than in other communities.

The research team on this project included:

Tanya R. Peckmann, Saint Mary's University (Halifax, Canada); Mary Manhein, Louisiana State University; Ginesse Listi, Louisiana State University; Michel Fournier, RCMP, Forensic Facial Identification Services (Fredericton, Canada)

Facial reconstruction is a method used in forensic anthropology to aid in the identification of skeletal remains. Contrary to what you might think, the objective isn't to produce a portrait of the person. The success is in reproducing the facial features based on the skull. The hoped for result is that once the photographs of the reconstruction are circulated, someone will recognize the person. On the other hand, the photographs may remind someone of a person they once knew and have not seen for a while. Before law enforcement can solve a crime, they must first know whom to look for so either circumstance may help establish an identity. The goal of facial reconstruction is to help find a connection between the bones and a person.

Tissue Depth Charts are important for a successful facial reconstruction as they determine the foundation of the head. Information about race, gender, age, and weight is matched with the information on tissue depth charts. From that starting point, the forensic artist creates an image of that person. Facial reconstructions for children are especially difficult. In the past, artists used facial growth patterns, as there was limited information on tissue depths. Establishing gender in children is still challenging, as there are few facial differences between males and female until they reach puberty. However, the newer studies with children are filling a gap in forensic information. Various studies indicate violence against children is increasing and the information gathered in the tissue depth studies will help make identification of children easier.

An artist will use all available information to add the features and final details to a reconstruction. The artist takes great care to follow the information gained from the skull. This may be the best, and last chance, this individual has of reclaiming their lost identity.

When working with Tissue Depth Charts the artist visualizes how the muscles, tendons, fat tissue, and skin will all come together on the foundation of the skull. Three-dimensional reconstructions are usually a last resort when there are no leads and no witnesses. The body may have decomposed, and there are not enough details to connect them with a known missing person.

The bones of the skull are a key factor in an individual's facial appearance. They form the framework to which all the muscles, tissue, fat and skin are attached. All humans have a similar appearance, it's the small differences that allow us to make identifications and recognize different individuals. In addition, each ethnic group has specific characteristics that apply to them alone.

Another approach to facial reconstruction is the Anatomical Method. German anatomist His (1895) was the first to record his scientific findings in this field. Along with anatomist Kollman, they worked to reconstruct the faces of several people including Johann Sebastian Bach (1685-1750), and Dante. Kollman also reconstructed the likeness of a stoneage woman from Auvenier, France (1898). On the Russian side, noted Russian Anthropologist, Mikhail Gerasimov (1907-1970), used his extensive anatomical research of muscles to develop the Anatomical Method in 1927. With this method, the seven structures that most define the outer surface of the face are sculpted onto the skull. The term 'structure' is used, as only four of the seven are muscles. The other three are important because they add substance to the face.

- Temporalis Muscle
- Zygomaticus Muscle
- Masseter Muscle
- Orbicularis Oris Muscle
- Parotid Gland
- Buccal Fatty Pad
- Fat Pad of the Chin

The variable size and thickness of muscles can have a significant impact on the outer appearance. Some anatomical training is important before attempting a reconstruction using this method alone.

In Europe, Richard Helmer followed the American Method. However, at Manchester University, Richard Neave developed a new method that combined both the Russian and American techniques to create a new procedure, which is widely used today. *Making Faces,* Prag & Neave (1997). The Manchester method relies heavily on anatomical information. With the American Method, the skill of the artist is more important to produce a successful reconstruction.

While the current methods of facial reconstruction are not perfect, the challenge is to continue to research and improve our knowledge of the skull, as well as, how to extract more information from the skull. Currently, a number of individuals are doing more research on tissue depths. The methods artists use to reconstruct a face may vary, but most tend to use a combination of methods. Most forensic artists believe that some knowledge of anatomy and facial muscles along with the Tissue Depths will produce the most accuracy.

We are not going to be working through a full facial reconstruction in this book. Rather, we will be learning to develop faces based on study skulls. If you have a study skull you may want to follow along and add the muscles as we work thorough the next chapter.

Learning about both the Tissue Depth Charts and the Anatomical method will give you a good idea of what goes into developing a facial reconstruction. You will learn which areas are notably different between the races as well as between male and female. You will also see how tissue depth changes if a person gains or loses weight. You can then apply that knowledge to your own sculptures. In Part Five we will apply the facial muscles, one by one, and check them against the tissue depth measurements for a Caucasian female of normal weight. You may want to highlight the section you are using. It's very easy to pick up the wrong number as you are working back and forth. Your faces will look different depending on the study skull you are starting with. I have included the Tissue Depth Charts for males and females, courtesy of Dr. Stanley Rhine (Figures 4-3, 4-4 and 4-5).

You may want to use your study skull to practice sculpting a variety of individuals. Of course, there will be differences between skulls, and the measurements will differ. However, the method of applying the clay and checking tissue depth will be the same. Use the correct measurements for the desired individual and use clay to add in the obvious differences. Specifically note the differences in the jaw line, brow ridge, nose, and chin between males and females.

If you were doing an actual reconstruction with a human skull, you would want to be very precise with your measurements and would have the tools necessary to do so. Using rulers divided in millimeters, you can get correct measurements even though they may not be perfect. You will learn which areas have the most and least flesh. Some forensic sculptors drill holes in the skull cast and insert tiny wooden "pegs" into the holes to achieve the exact depth. Others use vinyl erasers, cut to the correct depth, and glued onto the skull for markers.

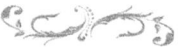

In addition to regular sculpting tools, I recommend a few other items. Top to bottom (Figure 4-1), I especially like small dividers. They are invaluable when working in small areas. Rulers, that measure in millimeters as well as inches. I

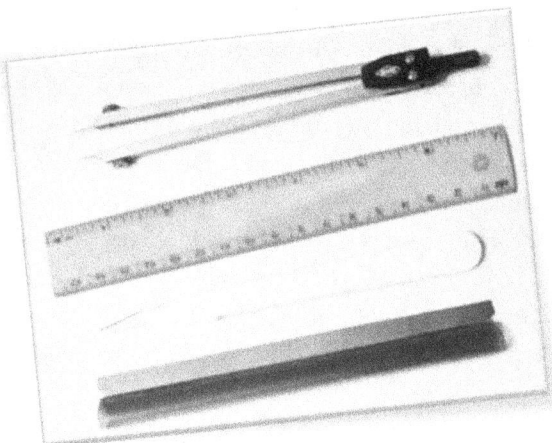

have several plastic ones in different lengths; they have a certain degree of flexibility that I like. I also like steel ones because they don't flex. Disposable scalpels, these are very sharp, delicate blades. You can purchase them at medical supply stores. Bottom, a clay blade, the kind made for polymer clay, available at any craft store.

Figure 4-1

Digital calipers (Figure 4-2) are not useful for everything but they do have advantages. The digital display will show both millimeters and inches so you don't have to guess or try to count millimeters on a ruler. You slide the 'case' back and forth and the measurement appears on the screen. Another neat use is the metal gauge on the opposite end. To determine depth, extend the metal tip, insert it into the clay, and read the correct measurement in the display.

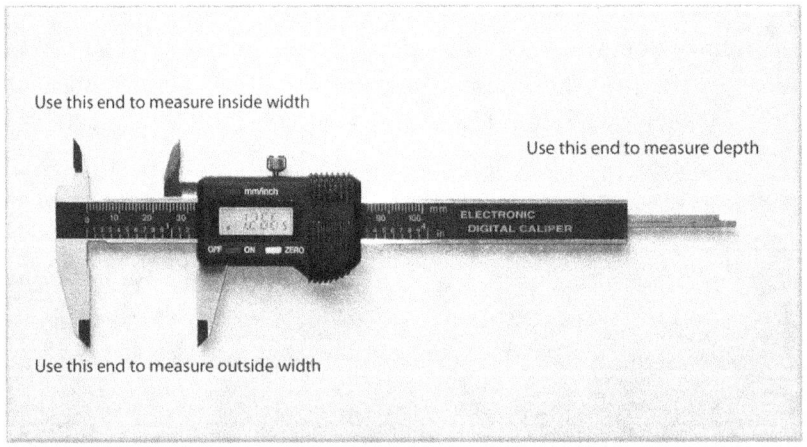

Figure 4-2

Tissue Depth Charts for Caucasoids (European Derived)

All measurements are in millimeters	Slender		Normal		Obese	
	Male	Female	Male	Female	Male	Female
Midline						
1. Supraglabella	2.25	2.50	4.25	3.50	5.50	4.25
2. Glabella	2.50	4.00	5.25	4.75	7.50	7.50
3. Nasion	4.25	5.25	6.50	5.50	7.50	7.00
4. End of nasals	2.50	2.25	3.00	2.75	3.50	4.25
5. Mid-philtrum	6.25	5.00	10.00	8.50	11.00	9.00
6. Upper lip margin	9.75[a]	6.25	9.75	9.00	11.00	11.00
7. Lower lip margin	9.50[a]	8.50	11.00	10.00	12.75	12.25
8. Chin-lip fold	8.75	9.25	10.75	9.50	12.25	13.75
9. Mental eminence	7.00	8.50	11.25	10.00	14.00	14.25
10. Beneath chin	4.50	3.75	7.25	5.75	10.75	9.00
Bilateral						
11. Frontal eminence	3.00	2.75	4.25	3.50	5.50	5.00
12. Supraorbital	6.25	5.25	8.25	7.00	10.25	10.00
13. Suborbital	2.75	4.00	5.75	6.00	8.25	8.50
14. Inferior malar	8.50	7.00	13.25	12.75	15.25	14.00
15. Lateral orbit	5.00	6.00	10.00	10.75	13.75	14.75
16. Zygomatic arch, halfway	3.00	3.50	7.25	7.50	11.75	13.00
17. Supraglenoid	4.25	4.25	8.50	8.00	11.25	10.50
18. Gonion	4.50	5.00	11.50	12.00[a]	17.50	17.50
19. Supra 2nd molar	12.00	12.00	19.50	19.25	25.00	23.75
20. Occlusal line	12.00	11.00	18.25	17.00	23.50	20.25
21. Sub 2nd molar	10.00	9.50[a]	16.00	15.50	19.75	18.75

Courtesy of Dr. Stanley Rhine 4-10

Figure 4-3

Tissue Depth Chart for American Negroids

All measurements are in millimeters	Slender		Normal		Obese	
	Male	Female	Male	Female	Male	Female
Midline						
1. Supraglabella	4.00	5.00	5.00	4.50	5.00	3.50
2. Glabella	5.25	6.00	6.25	6.00	7.50	6.00
3. Nasion	5.25	5.25	6.00	5.25	5.25	4.75
4. End of nasals	3.00	3.25	3.75	3.75	3.25	3.00
5. Mid-philtrum	11.75	10.00	12.25	11.25	11.75	12.00
6. Upper lip margin	12.50	12.00	14.25	12.50	12.50	15.25
7. Lower lip margin	13.75	12.25	15.50	15.00	15.50	12.00
8. Chin-lip fold	11.75	9.50	11.75	12.25	13.00	12.25
9. Mental eminence	11.25	11.00	11.50	12.50	15.25	13.00
10. Beneath chin	8.00	6.50	8.25	8.00	9.50	8.50
Bilateral						
11. Frontal eminence	3.75	3.25	5.00	4.00	5.50	5.00
12. Supraorbital	7.75	7.25	8.50	8.00	11.75	8.50
13. Suborbital	5.75	6.50	7.75	8.25	9.25	9.00
14. Inferior malar	14.00	14.50	16.50	16.75	17.50	18.75
15. Lateral orbit	10.50	12.00	13.25	13.00	20.00	12.75
16. Zygomatic arch, halfway	6.75	8.00	8.25	9.50	13.75	9.25
17. Supraglenoid	9.50	9.75	11.00	11.50	17.50	17.25
18. Gonion	11.50	11.00	13.00	13.50	24.00	17.50
19. Supra 2nd molar	19.00	20.50	23.00	20.25	24.00	23.50
20. Occlusal line	16.75	17.75	19.00	19.25	30.00	20.00
21. Sub 2nd molar	13.50	14.25	16.50	17.00	23.50	20.00

Rhine and Moore
Courtesy of Dr. Stanley Rhine 4/10

Figure 4-4

Tissue Depth Chart for Southwest American Indians
(Asian - Derived)

All measurements are in millimeters	Slender		Normal		Obese	
	Male	Female	Male	Female	Male	Female
Midline						
1. Supraglabella	5.75	4.00	5.00	4.50	4.50	4.25
2. Glabella	5.75	4.75	5.75	4.50	6.00	4.50
3. Nasion	5.75	6.50	6.86	7.00	6.50	5.00
4. End of nasals	2.75	2.50	3.50	2.50	3.25	3.25
5. Mid-philtrum	7.50	10.00	9.75	10.00	9.25	8.51
6. Upper lip margin	8.25	9.50	9.75	11.00	9.25	10.00
7. Lower lip margin	9.25	12.00	11.00	12.25	8.75	11.25
8. Chin-lip fold	8.50	9.00	11.50	10.00	9.75	11.00
9. Mental eminence	8.00	11.00	12.00	13.00	12.50	13.25
10. Beneath chin	5.25	8.00	8.00	8.00	8.00	7.75
Bilateral						
11. Frontal eminence	4.75	4.75	4.25	4.00	4.50	4.20
12. Supraorbital	6.75	5.00	9.00	8.50	8.50	8.25
13. Suborbital	3.75	3.25	7.50	6.25	7.75	6.75
14. Inferior malar	10.00	9.00	14.00	12.00	15.75	15.00
15. Lateral orbit	8.00	8.25	12.50	11.50	11.75	13.75
16. Zygomatic arch, midway	6.00	5.75	7.50	7.00	8.75	9.00
17. Supraglenoid	5.75	4.50	8.50	6.25	9.75	7.75
18. Gonion	7.75	6.25	13.25	10.50	15.40	12.75
19. Supra 2nd molar	14.25	11.75	21.50	18.00	23.50	19.00
20. Occlusal line	15.50	12.25	20.75	17.50	22.75	19.25
21. Sub 2nd molar	12.50	10.50	19.25	17.00	18.50	15.75

Courtesy Dr. Stanley Rhine 4/10

Figure 4-5

Marker Location Chart (Figure 4-6)

**The numbered locations correspond to the numbers on the
Tissue Depth Charts.
Markers #11 – 21 are Bi-lateral markers, one on each side.**

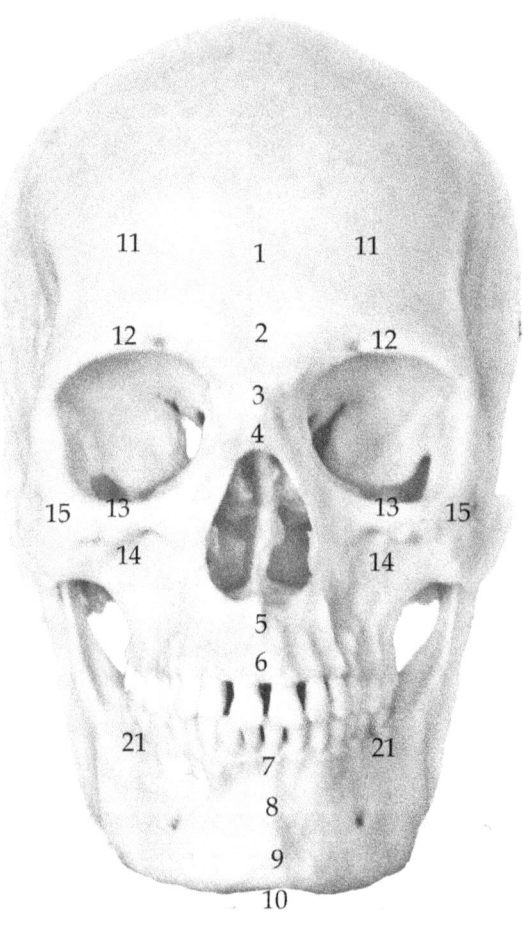

(Marker #10 is under the chin)

Figure 4-6

Marker Location Chart Profile (Figure 4-7)

**The numbered markers correspond to the numbers on the Tissue Depth Charts.
Markers #11-21 are Bi-lateral markers, one on each side.**

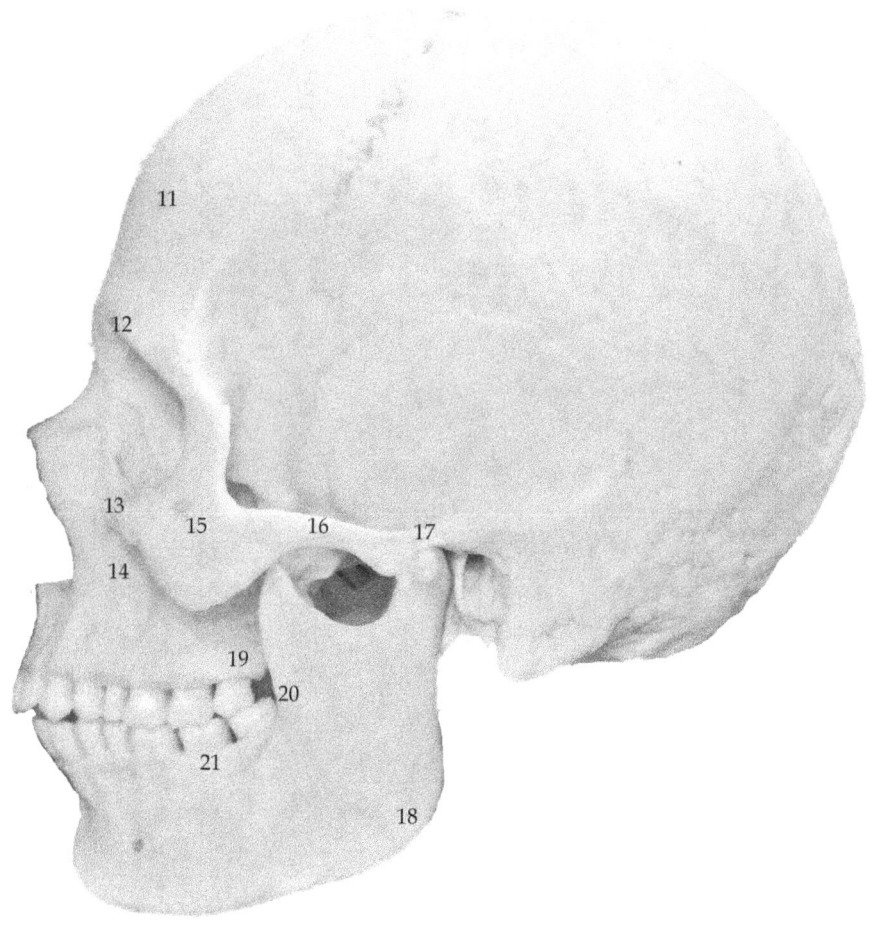

Figure 4-7

Part Five

Muscles of Expression

Muscles of Expression

*T*he brain sends a signal. The muscles of the face jump into action and deliver the required results. This process is the same for every voluntary and involuntary expression we use every day. The muscles contract and relax in response to nerve impulses enabling us to bring into being the expressions that make up so much of our nonverbal communication. The facial muscles, including the chewing muscles, are woven together in a complex criss-cross pattern. We can control a multitude of expressions by using the very fine, slender muscles lying just below the surface.

This is not an anatomy journal. I have tried to simplify the material into an informal, easy-to-understand order while keeping the important fundamentals. It will be easier to put it all together if you read this chapter first to get a feel for the material. As you become familiar with the facial muscles, you will acquire a better understanding of how they bring expressions to life (the "looks" that visually convey our moods and emotions). Over the course of a day, we may express happiness, surprise, joy, anger, or other emotions that will be evident on our face. We may not be aware of the changes in our own face, but definitely see them on others.

Expressions project an image to us. We might assume someone with deep smile lines around the mouth and laugh lines around the eyes is a happy person. We often find ourselves smiling simply in response to their appearance. The name for this is "mirroring", and is a technique used in marketing. Mirroring body language creates trust with another person. The other person sees you the same as them and are more receptive to you. Salespersons often copy body language to create a bond with a customer. This happens on an unconscious level and is a part of the brain that copies the action of other primates.

I took a one-day class several years ago where the instructor used what she called the "Monkey see, Monkey do" method. Rather than teaching a concept or technique, she sat opposite of us at the table and simply had us copy each step as she demonstrated it.

Auguste Rodin (1840-1917) has always been my favorite sculptor. I am inspired by the passion he had for the art of sculpture, as well as the emotion he was able to bring forth in his figures. In 1893, after the completion of *The Burghers of Calais* (1884-1892), he wrote in a letter to a friend, "I came gradually to the idea that sculptural expression is the essence of the art of statuary – expression through modeling". In this monumental sculpture, Rodin used facial expressions, along with posture and gestures, to portray the anguish the six Burghers of Calais felt upon their surrender to the English. In these close-up images of the head of Pierre de Wissant (Figures 5-1, 5-2), you can almost feel his despair and suffering, thinking these would be his last steps.

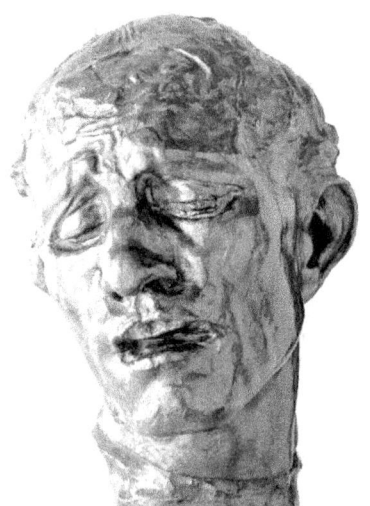

Figure 5-2

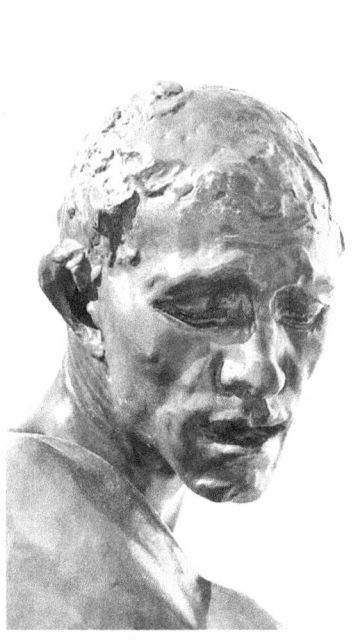

Detail of the head of Pierre de Wissant, from the **Burghers of Calais.** The final bronze sculpture measures 82.5"x95"x78".

Figure 5-*1*

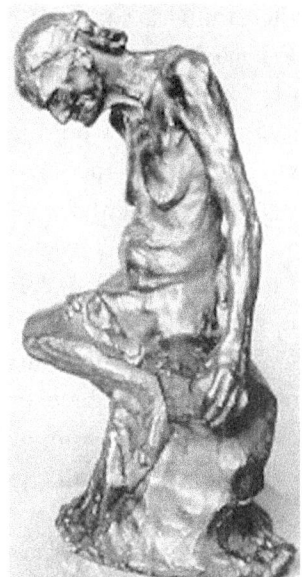

In a completely different vein and much smaller figure, only 20", is this sculpture *The Helmet-Maker's Wife* (Figure 5-3), also known as *She Who Was the Helmet-Maker's Beautiful Wife*, Rodin (1884-1885)

Figure 5-3

The 82-year-old woman who posed for Rodin was the mother of one of his Italian models. He said her decrepitude and character made her worthy of being sculpted and "…was an opportunity to depict the expressivity of the body even aged". The slumped posture, the bowed head and expression all work together to portray this sentiment. He later integrated it into the Gates of Hell to inspire reflections on the contrast between it and the graceful figures surrounding it.

These are only a couple of examples of great sculpture. You can find the history of these as well as the works of other great masters in your local library. Faces will appear cold and lifeless without some form of expression, even if it is so subtle as to go unnoticed. The great masters used that knowledge to produce sculptures that are still vital today.

If you ever have an opportunity to view famous sculptures, examine the details and note the fine points of expression. By studying the work of the masters, you will gain new insight about how the use of expression can make a good figure - a great figure.

Muscles are diligent workers, always ready to spring into action when they get a call from the brain. Muscles are fixed at one end. The end that pulls is attached to skin, or another muscle, which attaches to skin. Muscles have only one function and that is to pull, they cannot push. A rubber band is a good example of how a muscle works. Can you imagine pushing a rubber band to get it to stretch around something? No. We stretch it out then let it relax.

When a muscle contracts, it pulls the skin in the direction of where it attaches to the bone. This causes the skin of the face to fold in wrinkles and creases. Watch how your cheeks change when you smile. When I was a kid and made an "ugly" face, my Mother would tell me ..."your face is going to freeze that way". Did your Mother say the same thing? My face didn't freeze either, but in a way she was right. The skin covers an incredible degree of activity. The constant pulling and relaxing of a muscle will eventually cause a permanent line or wrinkle to form in that area of skin. Even though the face doesn't freeze immediately, using the same expression over and over for years will imprint that pattern on your face. A person who frowns frequently over a period of years may take on a permanent frowning expression, even though they may be a happy person. Squinting at the computer or against the sun are just a couple of other movements that can cause a frowning expression. This is one reason beauty magazines remind women not to frown or squint their eyes. Cosmetic companies make a fortune selling products to prevent or erase the effects of time. Botox is a protein that works to relax the contraction of muscles by blocking nerve impulses. Doctors use Botox injections to treat moderate to severe brow furrows, wrinkles, and facial creases. The injection paralyzes the muscle so it can no longer contract. As a result, the wrinkles relax and soften. The downside to this treatment is a person may also lose some ability to form other expressions.

One of my lesser talents is the ability to wiggle my ears. I've always been able to do it, and never thought about it until I read only 10-20% of the population can do this. It is the ability to control the **Auricular Muscles**. These muscles lie in front of, behind, and above the ear. They attach to the bones of the skull at one end and the skin around the ears at the other. Much like the ability to raise only one eyebrow, it is an inherent trait. Raising one eyebrow independent of the other is the ability to control the **Frontalis** muscles separately. The **Frontalis** is the large muscle of the forehead above the eyebrows, and is actually in two sections: a right, and a left.

Dr. Bridget Waller from the University of Portsmouth published a study on facial emotions, *Selection for Universal Facial Emotion*, in the American Psychological Association Journal (2008 Vol.8.No.3, p.435-439). Collaborating with anatomists, Dr. Waller examined the facial muscles on 18 cadavers. "Facial expression serves an essential function in society and may be a form of social bonding," Dr. Waller reported. "It allows us to synchronize our behavior and understand each other better." The results of the study found that all humans have a core set of five facial muscles, which they believe control our ability to produce a set of standard expressions, which convey anger, happiness, surprise, fear, sadness, and disgust. This study into the variations of muscles in the human face, and how this relates to facial expression, has important implications for our understanding of non-verbal communication. According to Dr. Waller, "Everyone communicates using a set of common signals. We would expect to find that the muscles do not vary among individuals. The results are surprising. In some individuals, we found only 60 percent of the available muscles". "The ability to produce subtly different variants of facial expressions may allow us to develop individual 'signatures' that are specific to certain individuals".

Dr. Waller continued, "There is a great deal of asymmetry in the face and the left side is generally more expressive than the right. But someone who is unable to raise one eyebrow without raising the other could in fact learn to raise just one." You might just learn a new trick as you go through the exercises in this section.

A muscle does not suddenly jump from a state of relaxation to one of full contraction. At any given time, some cells will be contracting, some relaxing, and some static. An expression is dependent on the force of the contraction. When you are sculpting, take into consideration, which muscles you would use to produce the expression you want, and to what degree. For example, a slight smile that only touches the corners of the mouth will not show much change on the upper face. A wide smile or a big laugh with the head thrown back and the mouth wide open will affect several areas.

The facial muscles used to form most expressions are those situated around the eyes, nose, and lips. I call them the expression muscles. The impact of these muscles is seen on the cheeks, forehead, and chin as you smile, frown, or display any of our other emotions. Make a slight smile, a wide smile, and then lift only one corner in a lop-sided smile. Flare your nostrils, squint your eyes, and look angry or sad. What expression do you want to sculpt?

Everyone has a preferred learning style. Knowing, and understanding, your own style helps you learn more effectively. You are familiar with the five senses or the five methods of perception: sight, hearing, taste, smell, and touch. I am a visual learner. I prefer to read instructions. You may be a tactile learner, learning faster by experimenting. Maybe you do better if someone demonstrates it to you. There is no one preferred style; however, science has proven that using more than one sense to learn new material will help imprint the information on your brain. In the following exercise, you will be using three senses (sight, hearing, and touch) to imprint the information. I can personally vouch for this process. I've passed many tests this way without resorting to memorizing material. I read the material first and then read it again aloud. I follow that with either writing down key phrases or using them to form a new sentence. This way a question asked in a different manner won't throw me. I have seen the material, heard it, and connected it to my brain in a tactile manner by writing it.

Practicing different expressions in front of a mirror is another good way to see firsthand which muscle does what. Hold your fingers over an area and make an expression. Try to locate the muscles used. Say the name of the muscle aloud while doing this exercise – even say what is happening. For example, place your fingers on your forehead; raise your eyebrows and say, "This is the Frontalis muscle. The Frontalis muscle lifts the eyebrows". Yes, I know, this is one of those things you do when no one else is home, or you can find a private place to practice.

Enlist your family to join you in practicing expressions and see how they look on different individuals. Kids love an excuse to make faces! Age, the degree of muscle tone and fat tissue will be different on each person so the expression might look a little different, but the muscles will still work the same. Have your camera ready so you can take close-up photographs of the different expressions. Your kids would love an Andy Warhol style collage of these on their bedroom wall.

Are you ready to learn about muscles?

You will not find a test at the end of this section. The real test is how well you understand the basic principles of muscles and can apply them to your own work.

History:

> In the first century, Greek physician Galen was considered the authority on human anatomy. He formulated his theories about human anatomy from his experience dissecting pigs as Greek and Roman law prohibited the dissection of humans. It was much later (in the 15th century) that Andreas Versalius came to believe it was necessary to examine real cadavers to learn about the human body. At age 29, he began human dissection in opposition to the Catholic Church and, in 1543, published *De Humani Corporis Fabrica, The Structure of the Human Body*. This was the first truly accurate presentation of human anatomy and became the basis for medical and healing practices. Fortunately, we have come a long way from that today. Scientists and Anthropologists have done the research, studied the results, and published their findings for everyone's benefit.

Anatomy:

Muscle is composed of cells. Cells are bound together into bundles. The bundles are then grouped together to form a muscle, which is covered with connective tissue. Muscles are fixed at one end. The other end (the moveable end) is attached to skin, or another muscle that attaches to skin. Muscles take different forms depending on how their "bundles" are arranged. Strap-like muscles have parallel bundles. When they contract, it gets shorter and larger in diameter. Unipennate (uni, meaning one, and pennate meaning a feather-like arrangement), Bipennate (two) and Multipennate (many) are diagonal bundles that pull at an angle. They do not pull as far as parallel muscles, but create more tension. Bundles that are arranged in ellipsis (more oval than round) around an opening are called Sphincter muscles.

This may look like a lot of material to absorb at once. As with anything, the more you work with it the easier it will become. Read the text, examine the pictures, study your own face in the mirror, and use the drawings to establish the location of each muscle. Not only do muscles control our expressions, they also contribute to the substance of the face, giving it shape and depth. Knowing how the muscles add shape and dimension to the face is a big part of sculpting life-like faces. It's the difference between just adding the features or a face that has believable bones and muscles. Figures 5-4 and 5-5 show the placement of the muscles we will be studying throughout this chapter. Figure 5-6 is an alphabetical listing of the muscles.

Facial muscles used for expression.

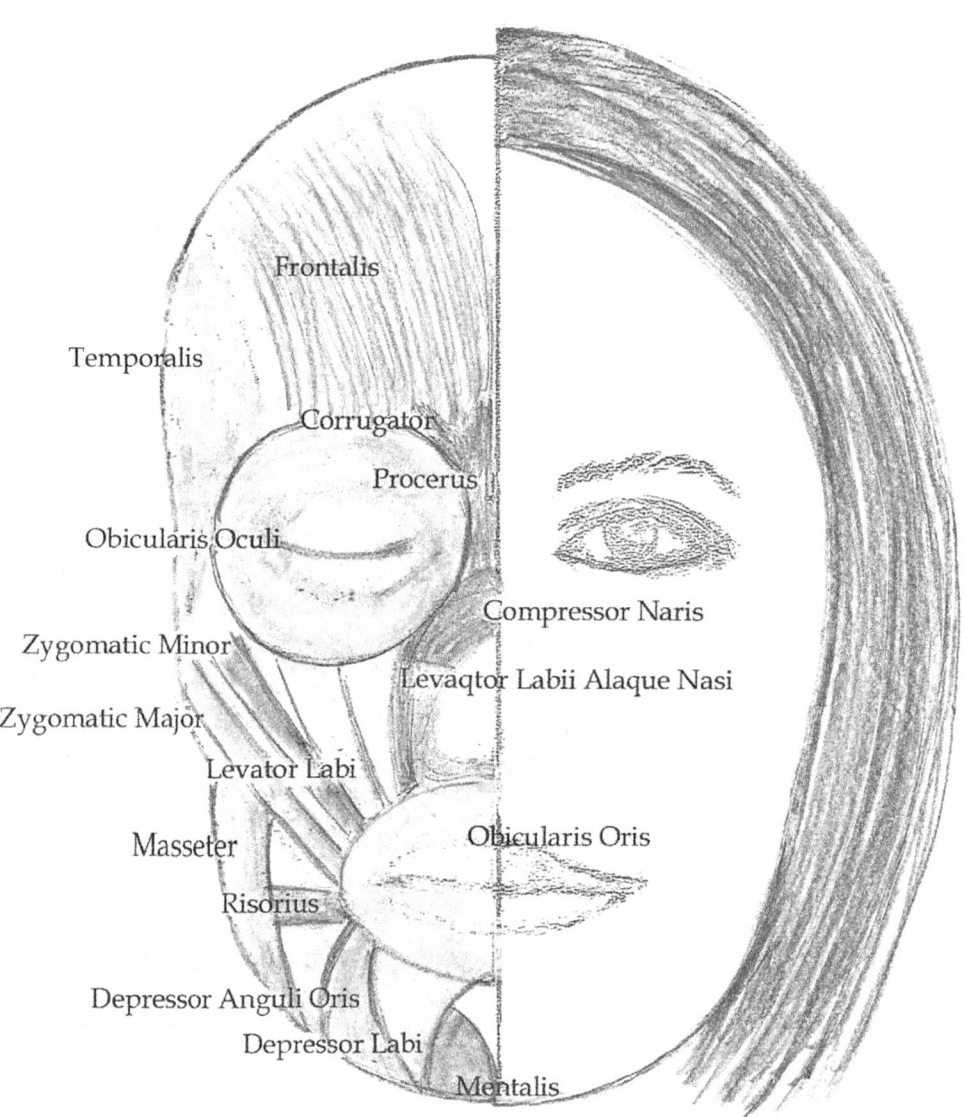

Figure 5-4

Facial Muscles Profile

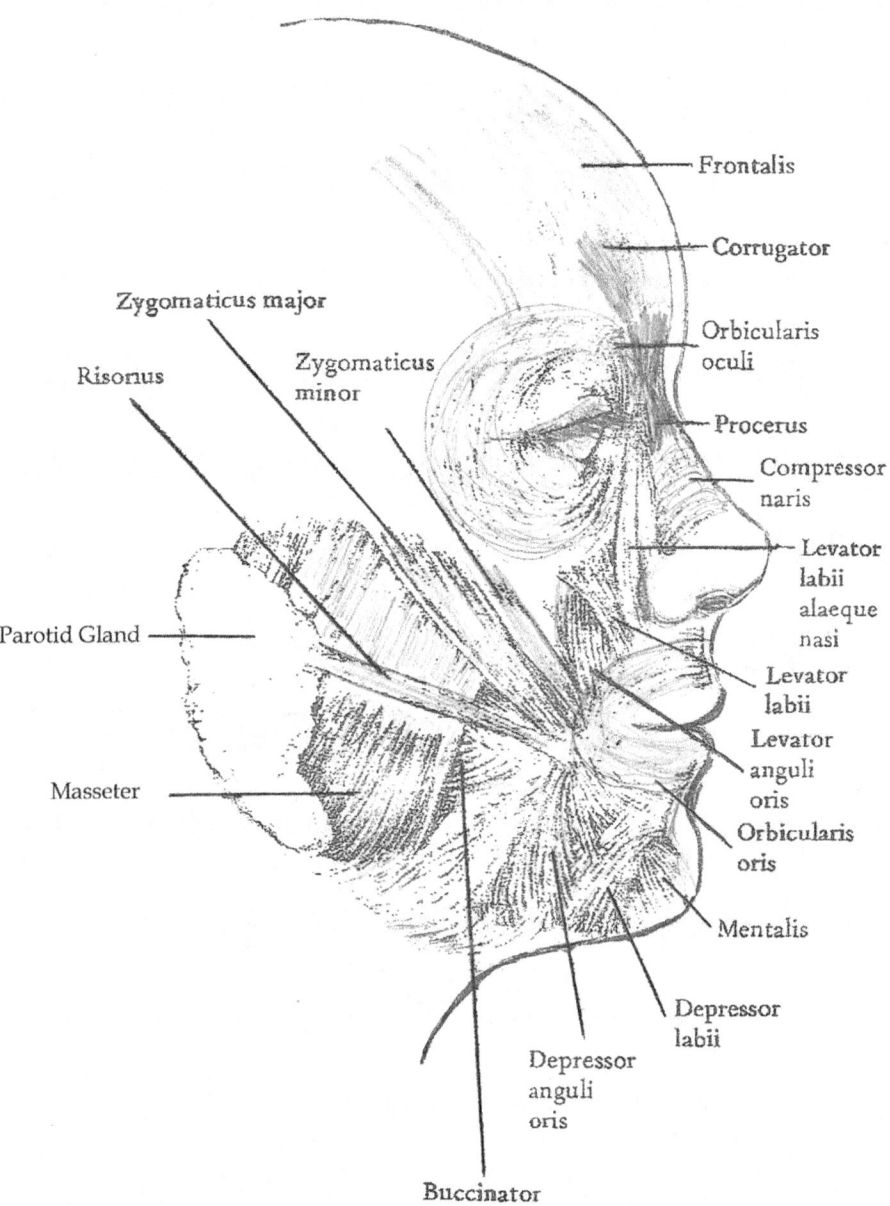

Figure 5-5

Alphabetical List of the Muscles (Figure 5-6)

Muscle	Location	Function
Buccinator	Side of jaw behind the Ramus	Presses the jaw against the teeth
Compressor Naris	Over the bridge of the nose	Lifts the back of the nostrils
Corrugator	The inner corner of the eyebrow	Pulls the eyebrows together
Depressor Anguli Oris	The chin, at the corner of the mouth	Pulls down the corner of the mouth
Depressr Labii	The chin overlaps the Mentalis.	Pulls down the lower lip
Frontalis	The forehead over the eyebrows	Raises the eyebrows
Levator Anguli Oris	Originates in the corner of the upper lip	Lifts the corner of the mouth
Levator Labii	Runs from the upper lip to the eye cavity	Lifts the upper lip, sneers
Levator Labii Alaque Nasi	Runs alongside the Nasal Bone	Lifts the upper lip and flares the nostrils
Masseter	The Ramus of the Mandible, runs diagonally	Holds the lower jaw tightly against the upper jaw
Mentalis	The chin, the fat pad in the center	Raises the lower lip and puckers the skin of the chin
Orbicularis Oculi	Below the Frontalis, encircling the eye cavity	Opens and closes the eyelids
Orbicularis Oris	Encircles the teeth forming the mouth and lips	Opens and closes the mouth
Procerus	Between the Nasal Bone and eyebrows	Pulls the inner corner of the eyebrows down
Risorius	The Masseter to the corner of the mouth	Pulls the corner of the mouth straight back
Temporalis	The area of the Temporal Bone to the Ramus	Pulls up the lower jaw
Zygomaticus Major	Zygomatic bone to the corner of the mouth	Lifts and draws the corner of the mouth up and to the side
Zygomaticus Minor	Above the Zygomatic Major, closer to the nose	Lifts the upper lip

When using a study skull, as we are here, there are a few preparations necessary prior to applying the clay. In an actual reconstruction, the artist might use prosthetic eyes or prefer to sculpt the eyes. For practice skulls, you may sculpt the eyes, use plastic, or glass eyes as I have here. The glass eyes are size 24mm and have a stem on the back, which makes them easier to apply. The human eyeball is approximately 25mm in diameter – or about the size of a quarter. The colored portion of the eye is 12mm. Figure 5-7 shows the eyes with the stem while Figure 5-8 shows the relationship of size to a quarter.

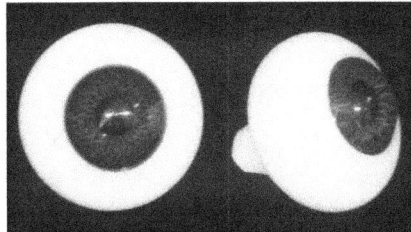

Figure 5-7

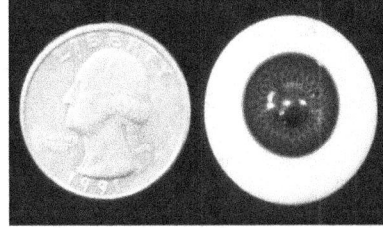

Figure 5-8

To prepare your study skull, pad the back of the orbital cavity with cotton. Then, cut short pieces of painters tape, and cover the cotton and the interior of the orbital cavity to close off any openings (Figure 5-9). On a real skull, this would protect the delicate bones of the orbital cavity. On your study skull, it makes removing the clay much easier.

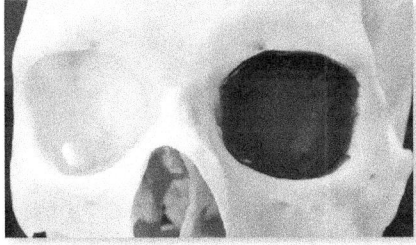

Figure 5-9

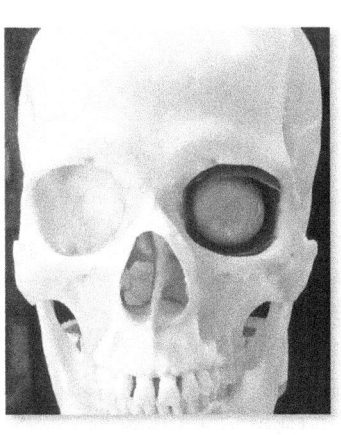

Figure 5-10

Place a small ball of clay in the back of the cavity to make it easier to situate the eye (Figure 5-10).

Before setting the eyeball in place, coil a roll of clay around the back as shown below (Figure 5-11). The roll of clay should surround the eye (Figure 5-12).

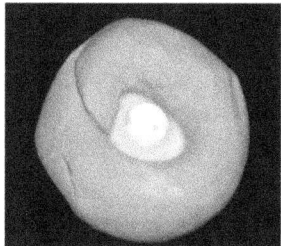

Figure 5-11

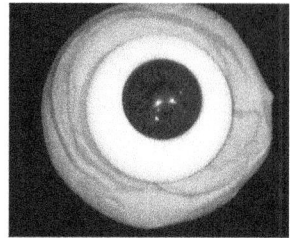

Figure 5-12

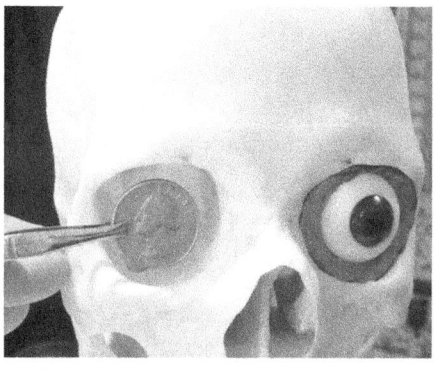

Figure 5-13

Place the eyeball in the center of the Orbital Cavity, similar to the position of the quarter (Figure 5-13). Align the eye so it is centered, and looking forward.

The eyeball should sit forward enough so that the cornea of the eye will touch a ruler held vertically, touching both the top and bottom of the orbital cavity (Figure 5-14). The lower edge of the ruler will angle in slightly, at the lower edge of the orbital cavity.

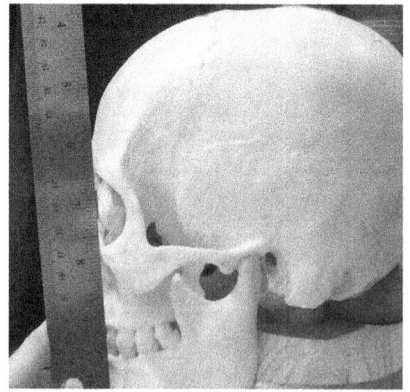

Figure 5-14

Muscles 101

Orbicularis Oculi (orbit=to go around and oculi=the eye) (Figures 5-15 and 5-16)

This wide, flat muscle encircles the eye and is a sphincter muscle, similar to the one encircling the mouth. It fits into the orbital cavity around the eyeball, extending up to the eyebrow and blending into the **Frontalis** and the **Corrugator**. It extends down to the zygomatic bone and out to the temporal region. The inner edges form the eyelids and the muscle contracts to close the lids. At the inner corner of the eye, the Palpebral Ligament interrupts the muscle. It anchors the corner of the eye to the bone and keeps the lid pulled towards the nose. If you rub the inner corner of your eye, you can feel this little ligament. At the outer corner of the eye, the muscle tucks into the side of the face creating a change of plane. The outer edge of the eye is on the change of plane formed as the zyogomatic arch curves around to meet the temporal bone.

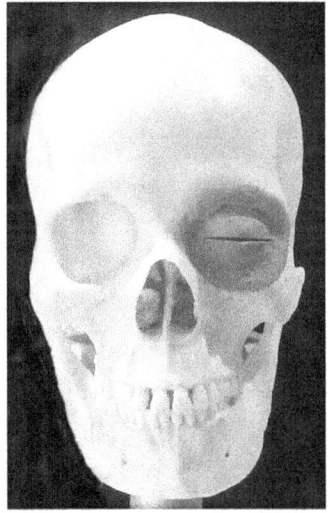

Figure 5-15
Orbicularis Oculi

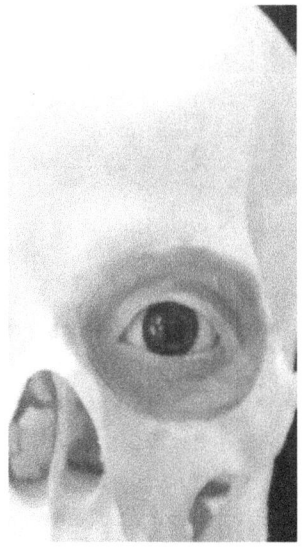

Figure 5-16
Eyelid opened

Temporalis   (Figure 5-17)

This fan-shaped muscle lies on the temporal bone at the side of the skull, starting behind the outer curve of the orbital bone and passing under the zygomatic arch. It works with the **Masseter** to pull the lower jaw up to the upper jaw with force, such as when you clench your teeth.

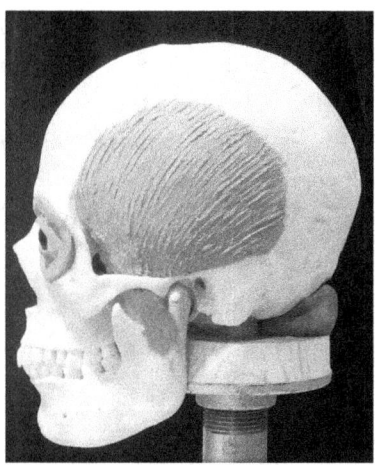

Figure 5-17
Temporalis Muscle

Orbicularis Oris (orbit=to go around and oris=oral)   (Figure 5-18 #1)

The **Orbicularis Oris** muscle encircles the mouth and is the Sphincter of the mouth. Its shape is more of an ellipse (more oval than round) than a circle. It has a free edge that forms the base for the lips and its job is to close the mouth. It can also protrude the lips, squeeze them together, and pull them tightly against the lips. Practice these movements to see how the mouth reacts each time. The **Orbicularis Oris** extends up to the base of the nose and down to the chin groove, halfway between the lower lip and the bottom of the chin.

Masseter   (Figure 5-18 #2)

The **Masseter** is a flat muscle that lies diagonally over the side of the jaw. It covers most of the ramus and attaches to the lower edge. It attaches to the zygomatic arch at the top and holds the lower jaw tightly against the upper jaw. The **Masseter** gives a curved shape to the side of the face, around the jaw area, and can often be seen on the surface. As a person ages, it can become more prominent.

Buccinator   (Figure 5-18 #3)

This is the broad, flat muscle on the side of the cheek. It joins with the **Orbicularis Oris** at the corner of the mouth. When you blow out, it stretches and when you suck your cheeks in, it contracts. It assists in chewing by keeping the cheek pulled in and against the teeth, and it adds bulk to the cheek area. If you have a flaw or separation in this muscle, it creates a dimple in the cheek.

1.   Orbicularis Oris
2.   Masseter
3.   Buccinator

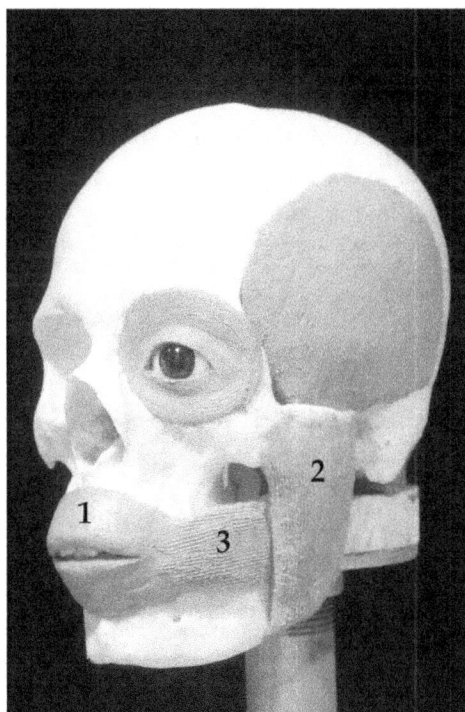

Figure 5-18

Mentalis, Depressor Labii and the Depressor Anguli Oris

These muscles (located on the chin) appear to run together, but are three individual muscles. Like all the muscles below the mid-point on the face, they are duplicated - one on each side. Sometimes slight variations on one side will contribute to a specific look of an individual.

Mentalis   (Figure 5-19 #1)

This is a cone shaped muscle between the lower lip and the bottom of the chin. It attaches inside and raises the lower lip. It also puckers the skin on the chin when you show doubt or disapproval. It sometimes appears as two round mounds on the front of the chin. If you have a dimple in your chin, it is because there is a cleft, or separation, between the two mounds that shape the chin.

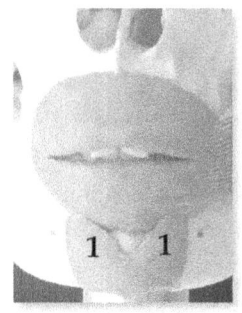

Figure 5-19

Depressor Labii   (Figure 5-20 #2)

This muscle begins at the lower edge of the jaw and attaches at the lower lip. Its function is to pull the lip down. We often see this as a curved muscle below the lower lip and above the chin.

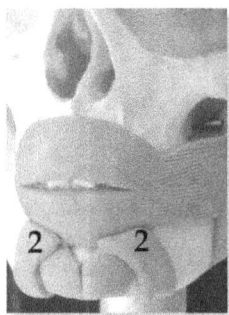

Figure 5-20

Depressor Anguli Oris (Figure 5-21 #3)

This muscle also begins at the lower jaw and attaches into the lower lip. It pulls the corner of the mouth down. Both the **Depressor Labii** and the **Depressor Anguli Oris** lie flat on the area of the chin that appears tucked in and under the corner of the lower lip.

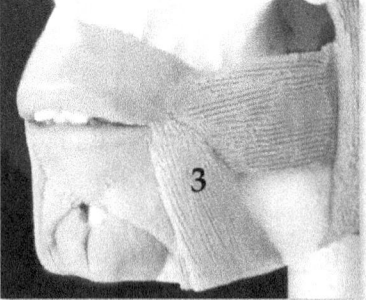

Figure 5-21

Risorius   (Figure 5-22 #1)

This strap-like muscle pulls the corner of the mouth straight back. It begins in the tough covering of the **Masseter** and inserts into the skin at the corners of the mouth.

Parotid Gland   (Figure 5-22 #2)

Even though the **Parotid Gland** is a salivary gland and not a muscle, it contributes to the curve and fullness of the cheek. It surrounds the angle of the jaw, lies partly on the **Masseter,** and produces saliva. Have you ever felt a twinge when you taste a sour lemon? That's the Parotid Gland. You can use small pieces of clay to simulate the gland as shown in (Figure 5-22) and smooth it with a sponge.

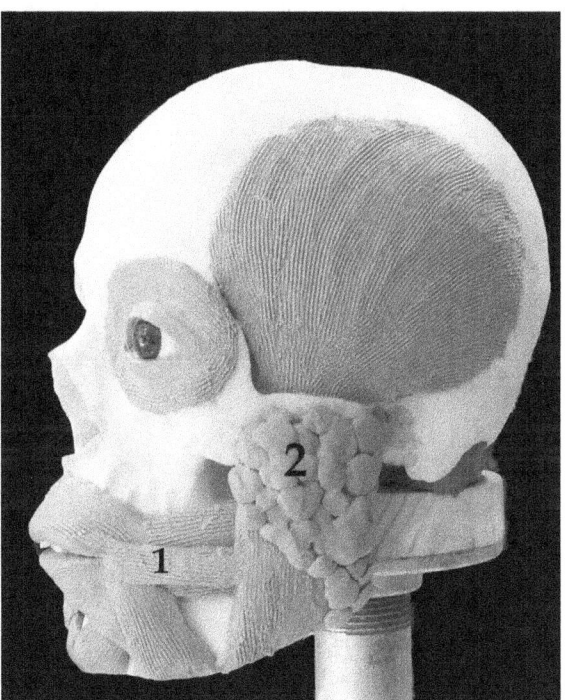

Figure 5-22

Levator Anguli Oris (Figure 5-23 #1)

This small triangular shaped muscle comes from the Maxilla and inserts into the angle where the **Orbicularis Oris** (at the corner of the mouth) meets the **Buccinator**. It lies under the **Levator Labii Superioris** and lifts the corner of the mouth.

Levator Labii (Figure 5-23 #2)

This muscle attaches on the upper front of the maxilla (under the orbital cavity) and blends into the **Orbicularis Oris**. The name **Levator** indicates its action; it lifts the lip.

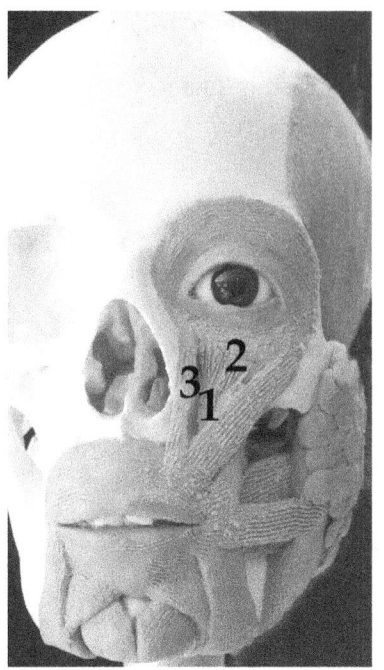

Figure 5-23

Levator Labii Alaque Nasi (Figure 5-23 #3)

The **Levator Labii Alaque Nasi** is a thin muscle that runs along the side of the nasal bone beneath the nostrils to connect with the **Orbicularis Oris**. Its function is to lift the lip and wings of the nose.

If you are an Elvis fan, you'll recall the slight lift at one corner of his upper lip that became his trademark. The **Levator Labii Alaque Nasi** is sometimes called the Elvis muscle.

Compressor Naris   (Figure 5-24 #1)

This thin, triangular muscle fits across the bridge of the nose, flares the nostril, and elevates the lip. Think how your nose reacts to a bad smell. That is the **Compressor Naris** in action.

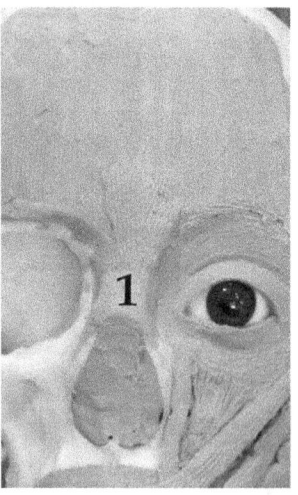

Figure 5-24

Zygomaticus Minor & Zygomaticus Major   (Figure 5-25 #1 & #2)

Both of these muscles aid in smiling. The **Zygomaticus Minor** runs from the zygomatic bone to the upper lip and lifts the lip. The **Zygomaticus Major** runs from the zygomatic bone to the corner of the mouth. It lifts and draws it to the side.

> Note: All of these small muscles cross over each other and may be difficult to distinguish individually.

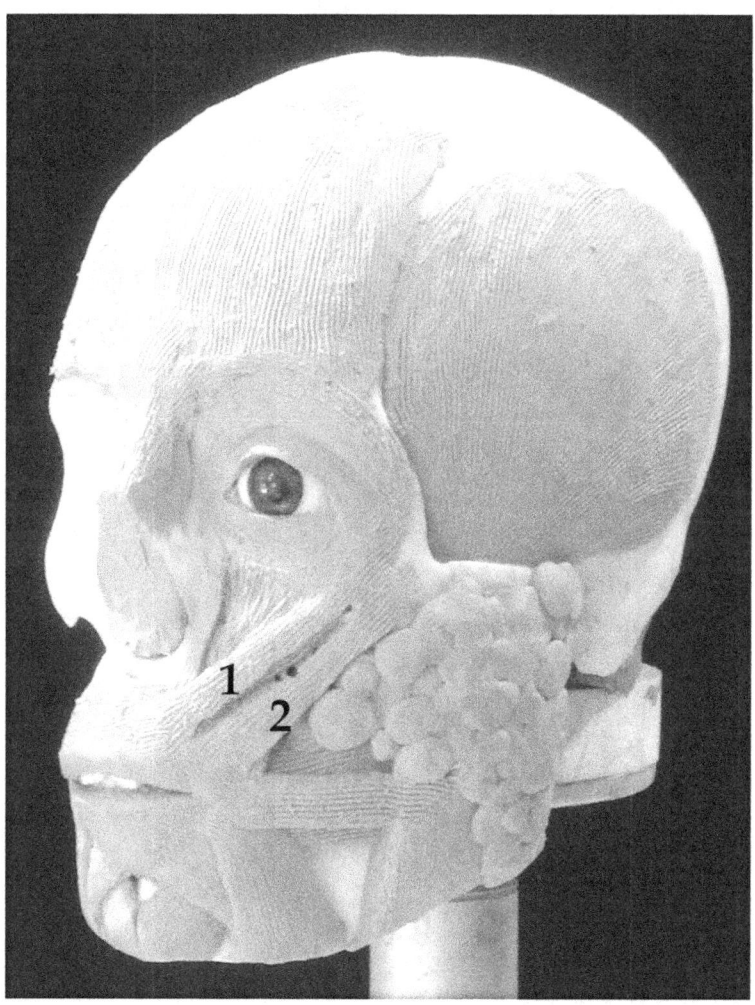

Figure 5-25

Frontalis   (Figure 5-26 and Figure 5-27 #2)

The **Frontalis** is actually two muscles that cover the entire forehead: one on each side. A flat muscle, it blends into the **Orbicularis Oculi** at the eyebrow and runs vertically up the forehead to the hairline. When it contracts, the eyebrows raise, the upper portion of the nose flattens, and the skin of the forehead creates horizontal folds. Raise your eyebrows in a surprised manner. You will see the **Frontalis** in action.

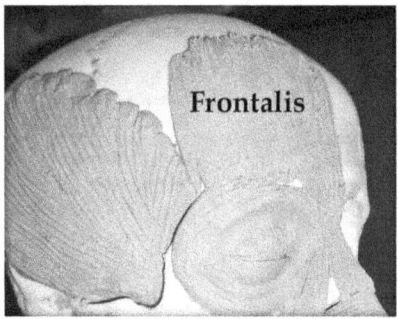

Figure 5-26

Corrugator (Figure 5-27 #1)

Just above the inner corner of the **Orbicularis Oculi** is the small, cone-shaped **Corrugator;** one on each side. When it contracts, it pulls the eyebrow towards the nose. The **Corrugator** is an adductor muscle. It pulls to the median line – to the center. This is what gives you the **vertical creases** at the top of the nose between the eyebrows. Pull your eyebrows together and note how the wrinkles form.

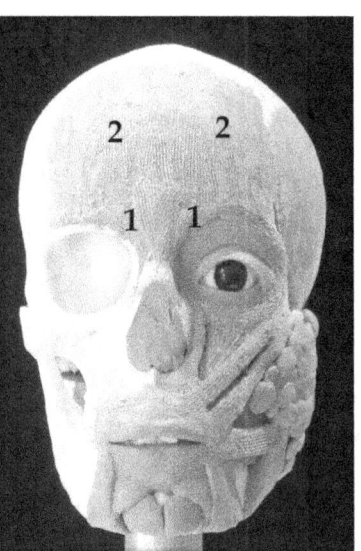

Figure 5-27

Procerus   (Figure 5-28 #1)

The **Procerus** is a slender muscle that lies between the **Frontalis** and the point where the nasal bone connects to the cartilage of the nose. When it contracts, it also pulls down the inner corner of the eyebrow and causes **horizontal wrinkles** across the upper part of the nose. The **Procerus** and the **Corrugator** are very close together, but perform different functions.

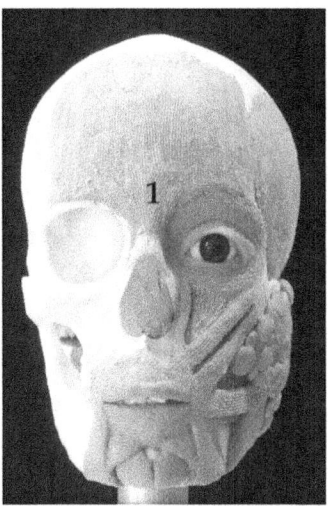

Figure 5-28

The **Procerus** in action

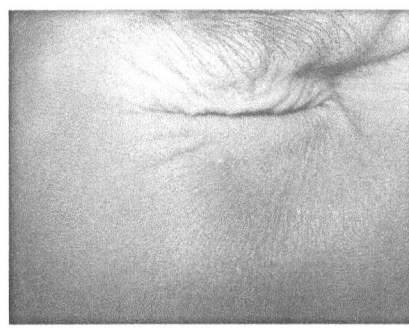

The **Procerus** muscle is also an adductor muscle. When you squint, the outer edge (along the side of the nose) pulls towards the nose and causes the skin to wrinkle into "crows-feet" (Figure 5-29).

Figure 5-29

If you are working with a study skull and have applied the muscles, you can now apply wide, thin strips of clay over the muscles to simulate the skin. You may need to add a little clay in spots where there would normally be fat tissue. You can cover the entire cranium with clay, however, I suggest leaving one side open to allow you to see the bones while you are learning. It's very hard to remember exactly where everything is once it's covered with clay.

This very interesting and informative web site, courtesy of Victoria Contreras Flores, shows the location and the action of each muscle. It you are having trouble visualizing the actions of the muscles, it may help to review them on-line.

http://www.artnatomia.net/uk/artnatomiaIng.html

Part Six

Proportions

Proportions

*L*earning to draw or sculpt realistic faces and figures takes time, practice, patience, and more practice. Understanding the structure of the human body is fundamental to creating figures that are life-like and realistic. Review the anatomical charts presented in this section, and refer to them when necessary.

Anatomical knowledge will give you a key starting point. The shape of the skull determines the contours of the face; ethnic differences will determine the shape of the orbital cavities, nasal bones, and cheekbones. Muscle and tissue will further shape the face, and the degree of fat under the skin will alter the face the public sees. If you have ever known someone who has gained or lost a lot of weight, you know some features may become more prominent and other less so. They will often look completely different. At least different in the way we see them because we are only able to see their outward appearance.

I have a friend I met when she was in her early 40's and who was "pleasingly plump", the customary euphemism for being slightly overweight. Several years later, she began to diet and exercise and lost the extra weight. When anyone commented on how different she looked, she would answer, "No. This is how I look". Her implication was what people saw when she was heavy wasn't the person she was inside. The extra weight had given her a different persona. When she lost the weight, she became herself again.

Let's talk about "rules-of-thumb". A rule-of-thumb is a guideline and gives you a quick reference when you don't have a live model available. There are many rules-of-thumb for sculpting and most of them are valid and useful. It is important to keep these in the context of guidelines and not gospel.

So where did this all begin? Years ago, people used different parts of the body for measuring. It was something they could relate to and was always handy. Although there are many measuring devices today, we still use some of these methods.

- Have you ever "walked off" a distance by using your feet - heel to toe? We consider 12" to be a foot, so I would think they must have used a man's foot to set this standard.

- You can quickly estimate the number of yards in a piece of fabric by holding one end in your outstretched hand and measure to your nose. For me, this is about 34", just short of one yard, which is 36".

- Artists often use their thumb to determine the proportion of one object in relation to another. To try this, hold your arm out with the thumb up. Squint one eye and measure an object by the size of your thumb. Move your hand over a bit and measure another object. You now have the proportional relationship between the two.

- We have raised and trained horses for many years and a quick way to measure the height of a horse is to use your hand.

A "hand" is the width of your palm, including the thumb, approximately 4". At some point in time, horse owners came to the agreement that 4" would be the standard hand measurement. You measure hands from the ground, up to the highest point on the horse's back. This is usually the withers (the point of the shoulder). For less than 1 hand, complete the measurement in 1" increments. Using this formula, a horse that is 15.2 would be 15 hands plus 2" or 62" tall at the withers (15x4"+2"= 62").

An interesting bit of trivia is that as of April 2010, there is a new record holder for the tallest horse in the world. He is Big Jake, a Belgian gelding. His official measurement is 20 hands, 2.75". This makes Big Jake 82.75" tall, just a quarter inch short of 6'11" at the withers! His neck and head will be above that point. I'm embarrassed to admit I need a bucket to get on my Arabian gelding Raquba, and he's a long way from 20 hands!

I'm always interested in how phrases such as a rule-of-thumb came into common usage. You can Google Rule-of-Thumb to read all the different versions. The most accepted version is that it derived from the Old English usage of the thumb as a measurement device, or rule. A more interesting version is that a man could beat his wife with a stick – so long as the stick was no thicker than his thumb. I think I'll stay with the first version.

You will often hear someone refer to a sculpture as being in the Classical Greek style. One modern sculptor, who sculpts in this style, is Bruno Luchessi. His books, *Terracotta, The Technique of Fired Clay Sculpture* (1977) and *Modeling the Head in Clay* (1979) both show wonderful examples of this type of work.

The human figure was a central theme in Greek Sculpture, and the science of proportions was considered the key to beauty. The Greek sculptor, Polyclitus, in the fifth century BC created a system of fixed ratios between the different parts of the body that was used as a model for several centuries. In a treatise (a detailed account) on his sculpture, the "Doryphorus" (Spearbearer), he wrote "...that beauty does not consist in the elements but in harmonious proportion of the parts, the proportion of one finger to the other, of all the fingers to the rest of the hand, of the rest of the hand to the wrist, of these to the forearm, of the forearm to the whole arm; of all parts to all others."

(As quoted by Erwin Panofsky, Meaning in Visual Arts, 1955)

The German Artist, Albrech Dürer (1471-1528), was greatly influenced by the Italian Renaissance artists and developed a compelling interest in the human form. He was recognized with establishing the measurements of the human body in his writings *The Four Books of Human Proportions,* published posthumously in 1528. His charts and drawings are still used today as the standard for proportional measurements for the human figure.

This brings us back to our original discussion of measurements and rules-of-thumb. The basic unit of measurement in figure drawing and sculpting today is the head. The standard measurement for a man is 8 heads and 7.5 heads for a woman.

Let's work through an example. Determine your desired height and divide it into eighths to find the proportional measurement. If you are sculpting a male figure, and the desired height is 36", divide 36 by 8. This will give you a "head" length of 4.5". If you look at the chart (Figure 6-1), you will see that from the top of the head to the chin is one head length, or for this example, 4.5". From the chin to the nipple line is a second head length, or another 4.5". Continue measuring this way down to the feet, for a total of eight heads or 36".

Here are a few other measurements using the head.

Females
- The body width = 2 heads
- Waist width = 1 head
- Buttocks = 1 ½ heads
- Bottom of knees = 2 heads from ground level

Males
- The body width = 2 1/3 heads
- Distance between nipples on chest = 1 head
- Head to crotch, the halfway point = 4 heads
- Bottom of knees = 2 heads from ground level

You can easily estimate proportions using your thumb as a guide. Holding your thumb up as described earlier, measure the head at a point on your thumb. Transfer that measurement to paper, and add seven more "heads" of the same length. You now have a figure, 8 heads tall, proportional to your original model. You can also purchase proportional calipers that figure the differences for you.

The Ideal Proportion Charts for Males and Females (Figures 6-1 and 6-2), are reprinted for your personal use from *Figure Drawing for All It's Worth* by Andrew Loomis. Written in 1943, The Andrew Loomis Collection is now in the public domain and you can access it on-line. I purchased my copy used, in 1984. Several books also include proportion charts for children. These are important if you do any work with children. A child's head will change several times as it goes through the growth process. As a child gets older, the head lengthens and develops more shape. The developing mandible is a noticeable difference, especially in boys.

Figure 6-1

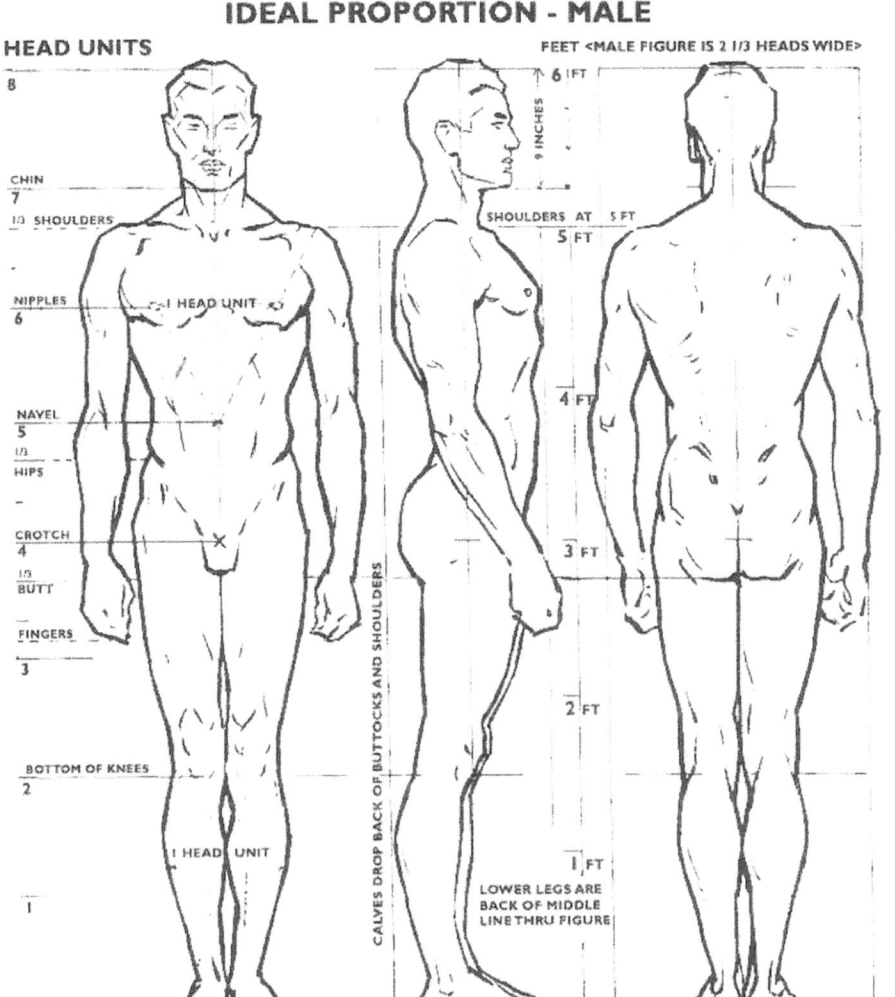

Figure 6-2

IDEAL PROPORTION - FEMALE

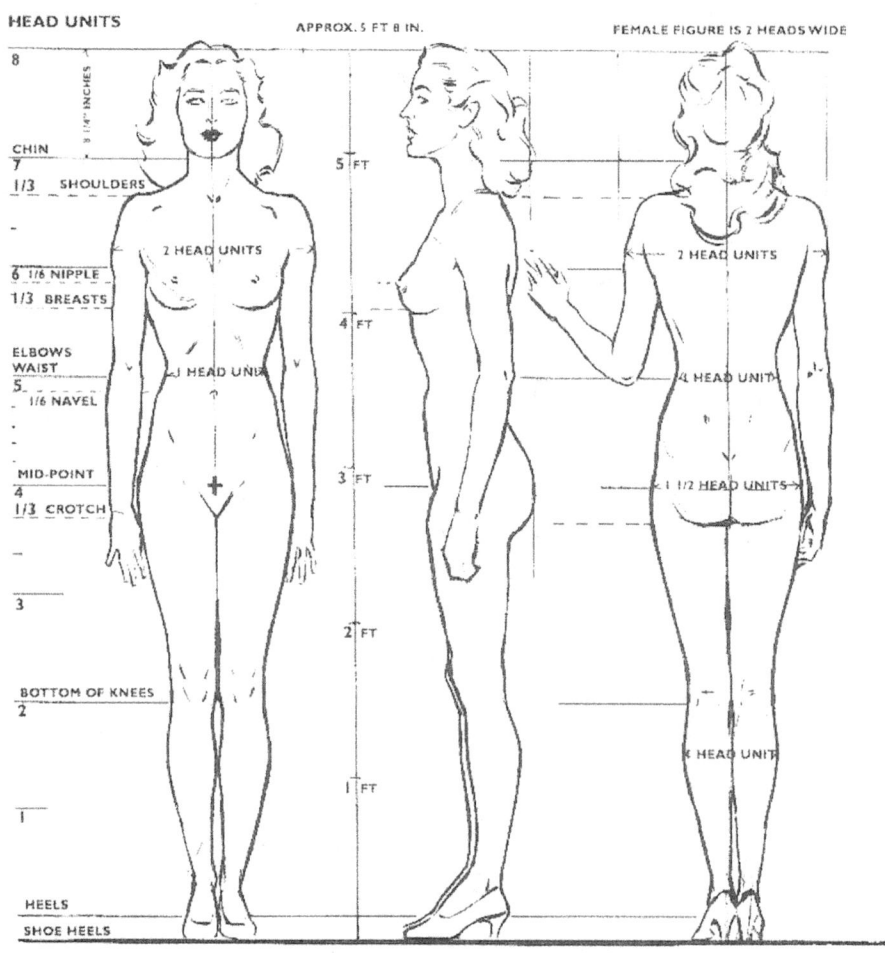

Many would-be artists choose to ignore the fundamentals of anatomy and they justify their mistakes as "their own personal style", but even caricatures and fantasy figures need a basis in correct anatomy to be believable. Have you ever looked at a sculpture and thought, something just wasn't right? It is usually because there is something off with the proportions. On the other hand, maybe you have a piece of your own work that doesn't look like you hoped it would. If so, step away from it for a few days. Review the ground rules of anatomy, and then when you take a fresh look, it will be easier to spot the problem.

We started this book with exercises to develop your Intelligent Observation. The ability to observe a person and recognize the individual differences that make that person unique is crucial to sculpting with realism. It is a study in real life. You are learning to be a better artist from the world around you. Observation alone, even intelligent observation, is not enough to allow you to immediately begin sculpting or drawing convincing portraits. Therefore, we studied the Bone Structure of the Skull, and the Muscles to learn what is below the surface.

It is the combination of recognizing what you see and having the anatomical knowledge to know the how, as well as, the why that produces that look. This is what gives you the tools to produce realistic life-like work.

Recognizing the facial dissimilarities between male and female is important, but it is only the outer shell. Knowing the foundation of the skull gives you the main pieces to the puzzle. Now you have the knowledge to begin sculpting from the inside out. Beginning with the foundation then adding believable bones and muscles, brings you to the exciting part that every artist loves - the features. The features are what make your sculpture come alive.

Jamie Salmon, is a self-taught contemporary sculptor who works in ultra-realism. His thoughts regarding his work closely resemble the ideas conveyed earlier in this book. Figures 6-3, 6-4 and 6-5, are examples of his sculpture. Take a few minutes to study the images then come back and re-read the following paragraph.

> "The most important part of the artistic process for me is the initial idea behind the work. If it isn`t as strong as possible, then the lengthy process of sculpting, moulding, painting etc, no matter how well done, will be for nothing and the work will fall flat. I want to make something that tells a

story or moves people in some sort of way, not something that just looks very real. Of course, I need my works to have a certain degree of reality about them, but it`s more of a heightened reality. This is also why I like to play with scale in a lot of my works as well. I think it is something that catches people off guard and forces them to confront their ideas about reality, and to think about the idea behind the work more deeply. Maybe more so than they would do if the piece were just life size."

Jamie Salmon, Avatar Sculpture Works (2010)

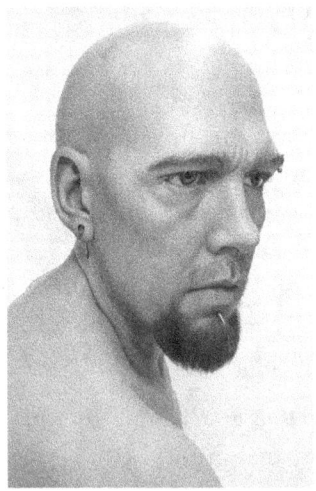

Figure 6-3

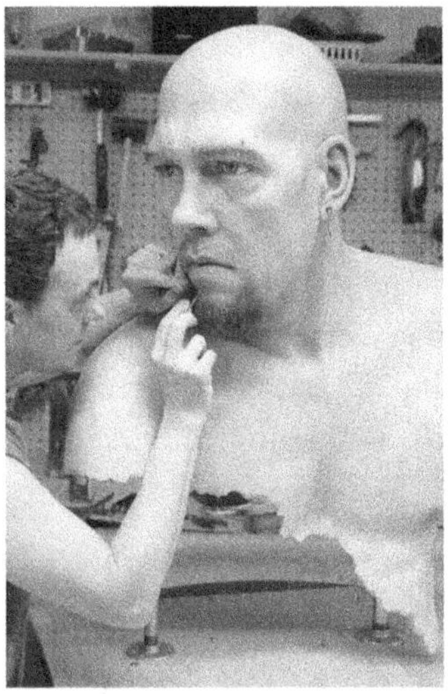

Figure 6-4

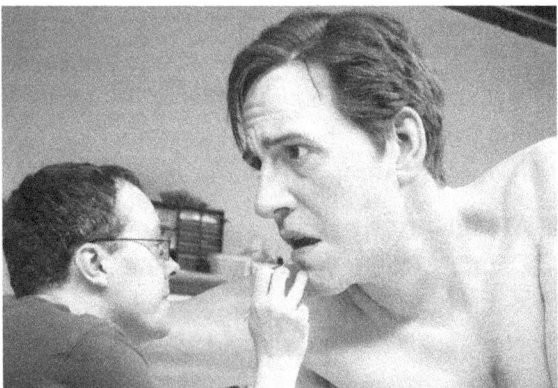

Figure 6-5

Images courtesy of Jamie Salmon

Part Seven

Features

Features

Primary Features

To develop a feel for sculpting or drawing realistic features, you need an awareness of how the features fit into the overall structure of the face. The surface can have many variables, but it will still be believable if the underlying foundation is correct. When you think of the face, most people think of the eyes, the nose, and the lips. I call these the primary features, the first ones noticed. The eyebrows, chin, and ears play a secondary role surrounding the primary features. Just as important but not as noticeable. Everyone's face, almost without exception, is a composite of imbalances. Different individuals will show a different composite. Some imbalances will be offset while others will be completely balanced by different ones.

> Symmetry, being the same on both sides, is the generally accepted concept of the standard for ideal beauty. It is rare though, to find anyone with true symmetrical features. Then again, it's the differences, the asymmetry, that makes faces so interesting and contribute to our own unique appearance.

The Eyes:

In a sculpture, as in life, the eyes are the most noticed feature of the face. Often called the window of the soul, many poems and songs have been written over the years eulogizing the eyes. Cosmetic companies continue to introduce products to enhance the beauty and seductive quality of the eyes. The nose might be a little off; the ears not quite symmetrical and other minor flaws may be thought of as individual variations. However, if the eyes are not centered and properly aligned, the viewer will notice it immediately. It may be artistically well done, but if not anatomically correct, it will fall short of the realism you are striving to attain.

What we call the eye is a simple name for a complex structure. Seven bones join to form the cone shaped orbital cavity (Figure 7-1). These bones protect the eyeball, which is centered within the orbital cavity. The eyelid and eyelashes provide further protection.

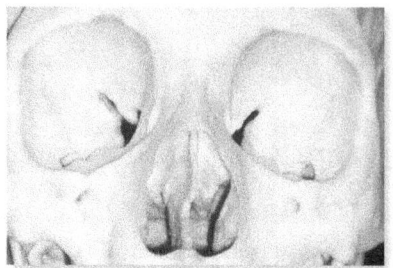

Figure 7-1

Six Extraocular muscles control the movement of the eyes. They connect to the front and the back of the cone-shaped orbital cavity. Like pulling the strings on a marionette, the muscles work together to keep the eyes in alignment as they change direction. In addition to the muscles; nerves, fluid, and blood vessels surround the eye. A layer of fat serves to cushion the eye if struck by an external object. As we get older and this layer of fat thins out, the eyes take on a sunken appearance and the bones of the orbital cavity become more prominent. This is often described as a skeletal appearance.

You may have seen tutorials, possibly taken a class, and been told the face is five eyes wide. What tutorials may neglect to tell you is that the two outer eyes lie on the area where the skull begins its curve to the back. This is where having a study skull is invaluable. You can prove this to yourself. Hold the skull about waist height and look straight down at the top. Observe how the curve of the brow bone (Figure 7-2) begins the change of plane between the front of the skull and the side. All the bones sweep back and around to the widest part of the skull before they begin to curve inward again.

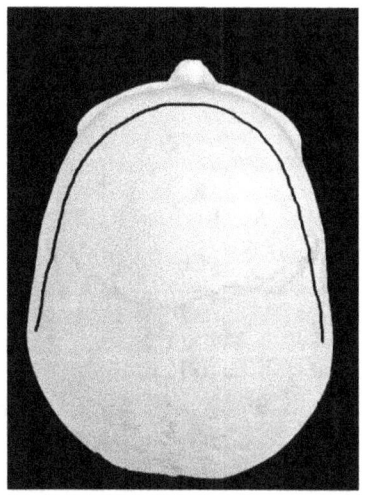

Figure 7-2

Many beginning artists use the rule-of-thumb of five eyes for the width of the face, without studying the anatomy of the skull. While it is technically correct, it often leads to a flat-face appearance. Figure 7-3 will help you visualize how the two 'outer eyes' do not lie flat on the front of the face but on the curve.

If you do not have a study skull ask a family member or friend to let you examine their head. Pictures of skulls are available in books and on-line but they will not have the 3-dimensional value of a study skull.

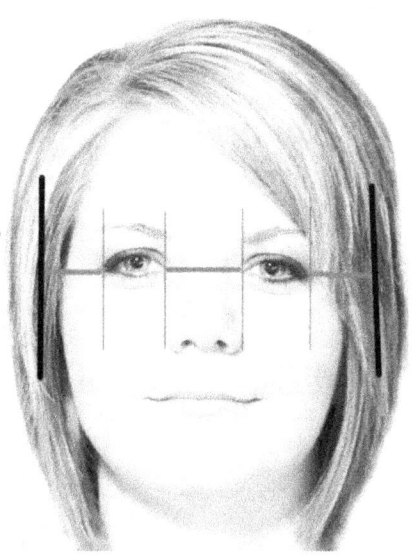

Figure 7- 3

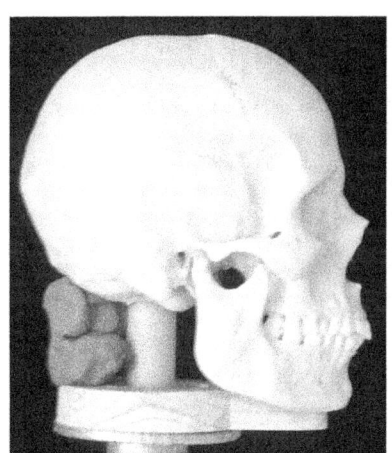

Figure 7-4

In this profile image (Figure 7-4), you can see both the inner edge (medial) and the outer edge (lateral) of the orbital cavity, **without having to turn the skull**. That's because the inner edge of the orbital cavity, closest to the nose, is more forward than the outer edge.

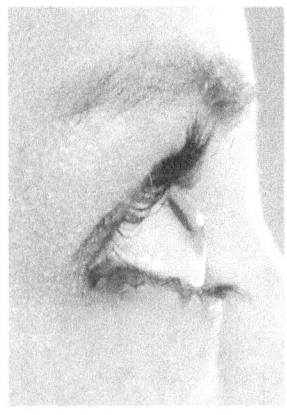

Figure 7-5

The eyes are more prominent and have more of a curve than you might think without knowing the anatomy of the skull. The opaque, white portion of the eye is the **Sclera**. It covers the optic nerve. The **Iris** is the colored ring of tissue that lies below the transparent cornea. It can be many colors and it is determined by genetics. Light enters the eye through the **Pupil**, which looks like a black "hole" in the center of the eye. The Iris and Pupil make up the colored portion of the eye, and are covered by a transparent dome called the **Cornea** (Figure 7-5).

The eyeball itself is 25mm in diameter; approximately 1" or the size of a quarter. There is a minimal difference in the size of the eyeball between the races. There is also a slight difference in the bony shape of the orbital cavity. No two skulls, however, will look exactly alike, even though they may be of the same race, gender, and age.

An interesting note about eyes: Mongoloids have the largest orbital cavity; Negroids the smallest and Caucasians fall in the middle. However, Caucasians have the largest eyeball; Negroids the smallest and Mongoloids fall in the middle.

Eyelids are thin folds of skin and muscle that cover the eyes. They help protect the eye from scratches and foreign objects. When we are awake, each time we blink the eyelids carry the secretions (tears) from the **Lacrimal Gland** (Figure 7-6) across the eyes. When we go to sleep the eyelids close to keep the eyeball moisturized.

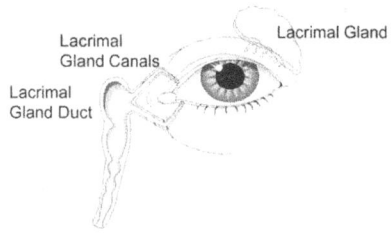

Figure 7-6

90

The upper and lower eyelids attach close to the tear ducts at the inner corner, the **Medial Canthus**. At the outer edge, the **Lateral Canthus**, they attach at a slightly higher point (Figure 7-7). Asian eyelids attach about 2mm higher than Caucasians and 5mm higher than Negroids. This is due to the shape of the lateral rim of the orbital cavity: the angular corners of Asians compared to the more rounded outer corner of Caucasians and Negroids. (Migliori & Gladstone 1984)

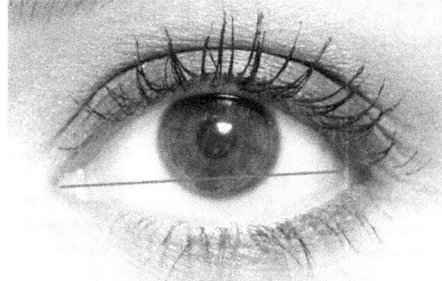

Figure 7-7

 The **Lacrimal Gland** constantly bathes the eye in tears that drain down into the tear ducts. If you think about it for a minute, it makes sense that the inner corner must be slightly lower than the outer corner. This allows the tears from the Lacrimal Gland to drain down, and be carried away through the tear ducts.

This small almond shaped gland is located in the outer portion of the upper lid, but is still contained within the orbital cavity. The Lacrimal Gland is responsible for the bulge in the upper lid. As the gland begins to atrophy, it's a little like letting the air out of a balloon. The tissue relaxes and the upper lid begins to sag.

The eyelids are actually several layers of skin, fat, and muscles. In a young person the fat and tissue over the gland, is smooth and firm. When you study older individuals or review pictures of older individuals, you will find the bulge has diminished, and is no longer firm. Artists are not always aware of the actual shape and fullness of the outer eyelid over the Lacrimal Gland. The area is convex, it curves out and back in. When sculpting, start with a roll of clay about half the width of the eye. The size will vary depending on the size of your figure. For life-size, I find a roll about the thickness of my finger is a good start. It's better to begin with too much clay and remove what you don't need, than to keep adding clay. You will get a smoother finish.

Compare this picture of my grandson (Figure 7-8), with the drawing of the Lacrimal Gland (Figure 7-9). If you traced the drawing over the picture there would be an almost exact matchup with the bulge in the upper lid.

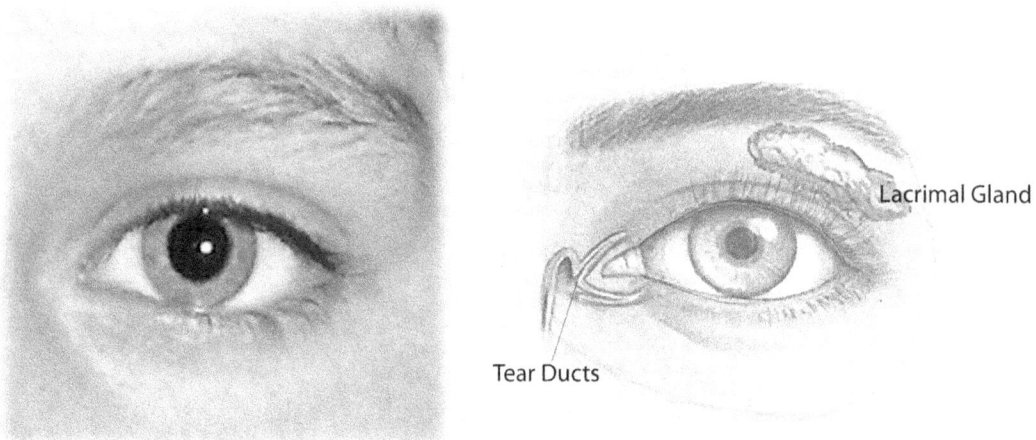

Figure 7-8   Figure 7-9

When you have an opportunity, observe eyelids carefully. They have a thickness to them (Figure 7-10). Do not make the mistake of making them paper-thin. When the eyes change direction, the shape of the upper lid will also change to cover the dome of the cornea. For eyes to look realistic, the lid must curve around and hug the eyeball. There is no separation between the eyeball and the eyelid.

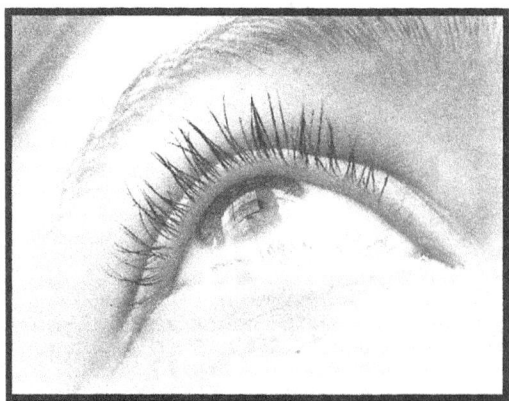

Figure 7-10

The upper lid continues up to the eyebrow and the lower lid joins the cheek area. The upper lid retracts when open and comes down to meet the lower lid when it is closed. When open the lid forms an upward curve (Figure 7-11). When closed the curve is reversed (Figure 7-12).

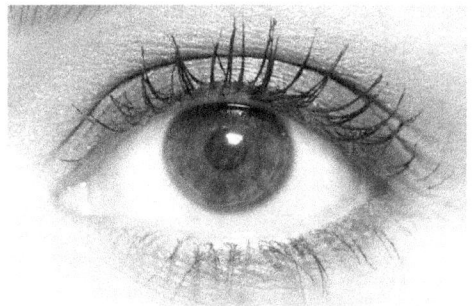

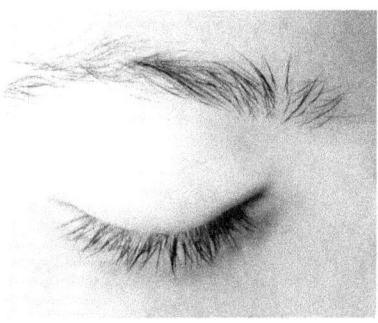

Figure 7-11   Figure 7-12

The highest point of the upper lid is closer to the Medial Canthus, the inner corner of the eye. The lowest point of the lower lid is closer to the Lateral Canthus, the outer corner (Figure 7-13).

The width of the eyelid opening is approximately 60% of the width of the orbital cavity.

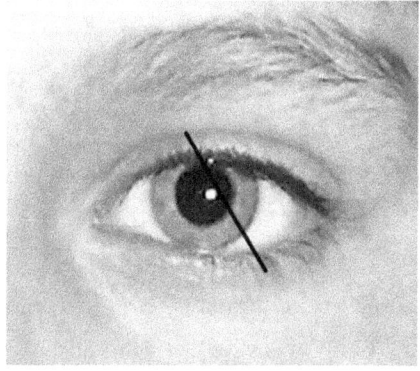

Figure 7-13

The eyes are neither round nor oval. Similar to a trapezoid, the shape is more oblique (at an angle or slanting).

If you are adding the eyelids separately as opposed to starting from the Orbicularis Oculi, place the lower lid first. You may need to adjust it several times to get the right fit. Begin at the **Lateral Canthus**, the outer corner, and press gently so the lid hugs the eyeball as you wrap it around to the **Medial Canthus** where it creates a slight s-shaped curve (Figure 7-14). The lower lid crosses, or is slightly below the bottom of the Iris. Use a sharp knife to trim the inner corner.

The upper lid is longer and more arched than the lower lid. It should rest at the halfway point between the pupil and upper edge of the iris. Placing them higher will result in a surprised look, too low will give a sleepy look. The upper lid overlaps the lower lid at the outer corner, the Lateral Canthus (Figure 7-15). Begin at the outer corner and gently hug the eyeball as it wraps around to the Medial Canthus. At the inner corner, the lid comes slightly away, and over, the **Caruncle** to meet the lower lid.

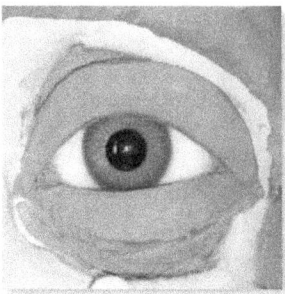

Figure 7-14

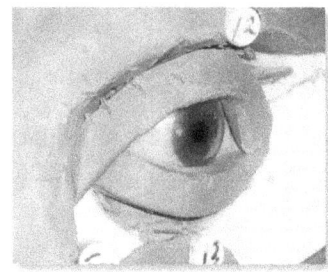

Figure 7-15

Once you are satisfied with the fit, place a tiny ball of clay in the inner corner to simulate the pink tissue of the **Caruncle** (Figure 7-16), and with the tip of a small tool push it into position. If you are working with small figures, remember to use very small tools to get the best results.

The **Caruncle** is the small pink portion of tissue in the inner corner of the eye that contains sebaceous and sweat glands that produce thick secretions. If you have sleep in your eyes in the morning, it's the substance produced by the Caruncle. It lies **inside** the inner corner of the lids and at the **edge** of the eyeball. It is not part of the lid or the eyeball. If the clay works its way too far up onto the eyeball, use a small tool to either remove some of the clay or push it back into position.

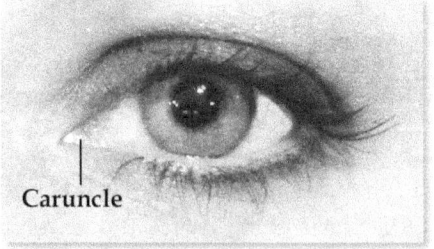

Figure 7-16

Once you are satisfied with the placement of the lids, check to ensure the entire eye area falls within the orbital cavity. If you have left the outer rim free of clay, it's easier to see. Continue to add shape to the eyelids with some fat pads over the lids and around the outer portion of the lids. Add the crease in the upper lid, about ¼" above the edge of the upper lid. Smooth the clay and continue to shape the eyes and eyelids.

Once the eyes are set it's time to stop sculpting. Step back, and evaluate your work. The eyes are very important. Examine them carefully with a magnifying glass and/or by turning it to a mirror and checking the reflection. Are the eyes level on the face? Are they tracking in the same direction? Did you position the lids correctly with the upper lid overlapping the lower? Review the facts on eyes on the preceding pages to ensure you catch any mistakes.

Have someone take a close-up picture of your eyes, for a study guide. Enlarge them on a copier so you can see all the details. Use a magnifying glass to study someone else's eyes.

The inner corner of the eye is always more forward than the outer corner. When the clay is warm, it's easy for the eyeball to sink into the clay while you are working. If you find the area near the nose is too deep, now is the time to remove the eye and start over. I have found that removing and resetting the eye actually saves time and produces a better result than if I try to "fix" it. You may need to add some firm clay beneath it, and put it in a cool spot to firm up before continuing. If the clay becomes sticky and too soft to work with, place it in the refrigerator for a while. If there is not enough room, or your family objects to a head in the fridge, a picnic cooler with an ice pack works fine. I will have to admit it's a strange feeling, even for me, to open the cooler and look down on a very realistic head.

A trick I use when looking at a sculpt in the mirror is to put a toothpick in every area that needs more work. This way, when I turn it around I don't have to remember if it was the left side or the right side. You can even draw a circle around an area you want to change. Our eyes sometimes deceive us when we see it in reverse, so the toothpicks serve as a marker for areas that need attention. We are working with eyes here but this is also a good way to check the shape and level of all the features. Remember, this is just clay. You can smash it up and start over as many times as you like while you are learning. I suggest stopping often to take pictures. It can get discouraging at times and with pictures, you have a visual record of your progress. I love digital cameras. They offer instant feedback and a quick way to check your sculpture. Your eyes will pick up errors in a picture that were not immediately apparent. Similar to seeing your work reversed in a mirror, or looking at it upside down, a two-dimensional image allows a different part of your brain to take over.

Walk away from your work now, and go do something else for a while. When you return, let your first glance tell you if it looks good or if something is a little off. If so, identify the problem and fix it now. I turn my sculpting stand towards the door. Each time I walk past I glance in and if something catches my eye, I can correct it. When I walk past and I am pleased with what I see, then it is time to move to next step.

You can add some fine brow hairs to help you visualize the finished eye. The brow tucks slightly under the brow ridge at the inner corner and continues along the brow bone to the outer end. Use a fine, sharp tool to add individual hairs in the direction of growth. For a more defined brow, add a small roll of clay. Men especially have thicker, sometimes very bushy brows. You will need to add clay to get the right definition. In general, female brows will be a little thinner and a little higher than males, especially at the outer end. Women will often have their brows plucked in the manner in fashion at the time, and cosmetics can alter the shape of the brow. Unless you are sculpting a fantasy figure stay close to the actual structure of the brow bone for realism.

On a reconstruction, the forensic artist has no way of knowing what the actual brows looked like so they use a basic form following the line of the brow bone.

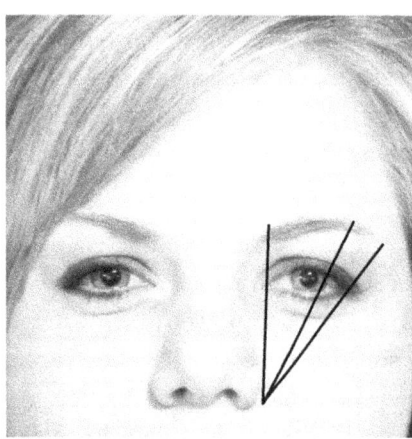

An old beauty axiom for females still holds true today. Draw an imaginary line vertically along the wing of the nose. Where it crosses the brow bone is where the hairs of the brow should begin. Draw another line diagonally from the wing of the nose along the outside edge of the iris. Where it crosses the brow will be the highest point of the arch. Move the line out further to the corner of the eye, and where it crosses the brow will be the ending point (Figure 7-17).

Figure 7-17

In a sculpture, as in person, the eyes are the most noticed feature of the face. It is imperative to center and align them correctly. Forensic artists use prosthetic eyes or sometimes glass or plastic eyes made for dolls. Doll eyes are not always symmetrical. Sometimes you will have to sort through several pairs to find two that match. I find you get better matches with the better quality eyes. If you have problems getting a pair that match, use a little paint to make the corrections. For sculpted eyes, you can incise the pupils into the clay. Ensure they are both the same size and aligned correctly.

Once the eyes are set, you can begin to smooth the clay in this area. Use either tools or your fingers, but maintain a light pressure. You do not want to mess up what you have worked so hard on.

Don't be overly concerned with how artistic it looks at this point. Working with a study skull your primary objective is to learn the anatomical features. Oil base clay does not lend itself to a glass smooth finish and the temperature in your working area can make it too sticky or too firm to work with. Always double check that both eyes are tracking the same direction. If you are painting eyes, check that the highlights in both eyes are in the same location.

When you begin to sculpt the eyes keep in mind the overall age of your figure. The eyes in a younger person will be set a little more forward, be more open, look more alert and the area surrounding the eye is fuller and smoother. Heavy sagging lids on a younger person would be quite out of place.

The current teaching is that the eyeball is situated level in the center of the orbital cavity regardless of its shape or size. More recently, a small study suggested that the eyeball is actually closer to the roof of the orbital cavity, and the lateral orbital wall than previously thought. A larger study was completed and the results were confirmed to be the same. The study found the median change is 1.4mm higher; and 2.3mm closer, to the lateral wall (the outer edge) than was previously thought. The projection is that the values would be identical in living individuals. *Journal of Forensic Science,* Vol.64, Issue 2, p267-269, March2009.

Continuing research into the area of facial reconstruction provides new data constantly. For your purpose in developing sculptures with more realistic details, the information presented earlier in the book is correct to use.

Individuals of Asian ancestry will have a broader, rounder face with a flatter profile. The nasal bone is flatter with more bony width between the eyes than Caucasians or Negroids. The general shape of the orbital cavity is rounded and non-sloping. The shape of the skull primarily explains the angular corners of Asian eyelids, compared to the rounded outer corner of Caucasians and Negroids, according to Migliori & Gladstone (1984). The fat pad in the upper eyelid is thicker than Caucasians and projects lower into the eyelid making it appear puffier. A defining characteristic of Asian ancestry is the **Epicanthic Fold** in the eyelid.

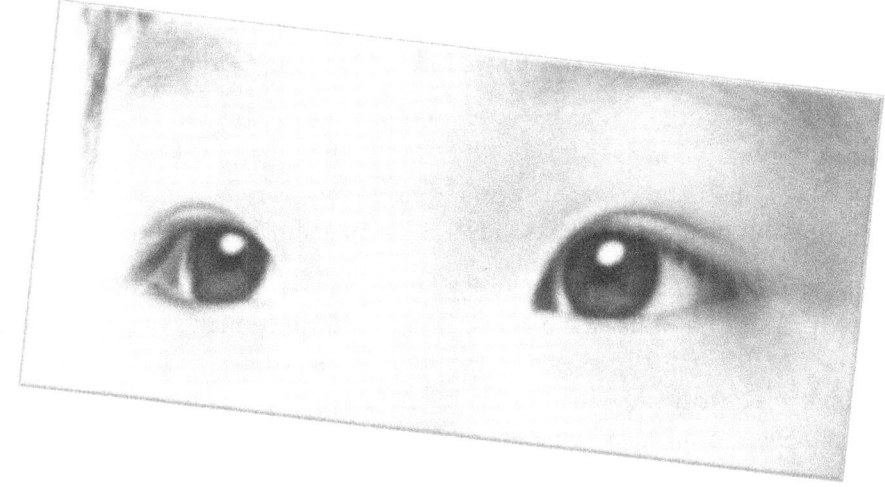

Figure 7-18

The **Epicanthic Fold is a crescent shaped, vertical skin fold of the upper lid. It extends out from the bridge of the nose and covers the Medial Canthus,** the inner corner of the eye. This trait is usually associated with Asians; however, as we saw earlier other ethnic groups can share this trait. This photograph of an Asian child (Figure 7-18), displays the broad, flat nasal area and the skin fold that forms the Epicanthic Fold. The bulge of the **Lacrimal Gland** is still apparent in the outer portion of the upper eyelid. The eyelashes of Asian individuals bend downward, which gives the appearance of even less space between the upper and lower lids. The visible crease seen here makes this a "double eyelid". Approximately 50% of Asians exhibit a double eyelid; the other 50% have a single eyelid.

The Epicanthic Fold seen here (Figure 7-19), is called a "single eyelid" as there is no **visible** crease. That doesn't mean there isn't a crease – just that it isn't visible under the fold.

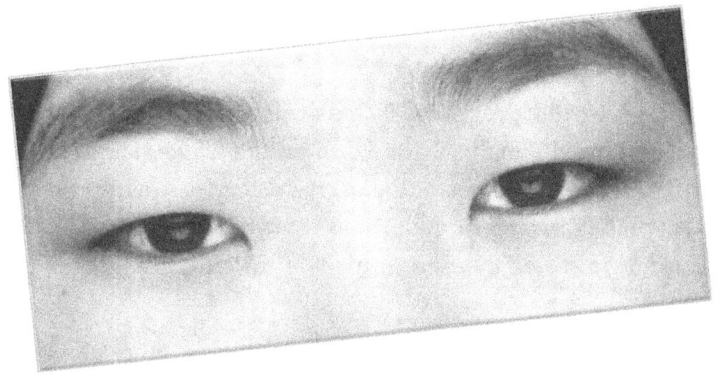

Figure 7-19

Figure 7-20 is another variation of the Epicanthic Fold with a double eyelid.

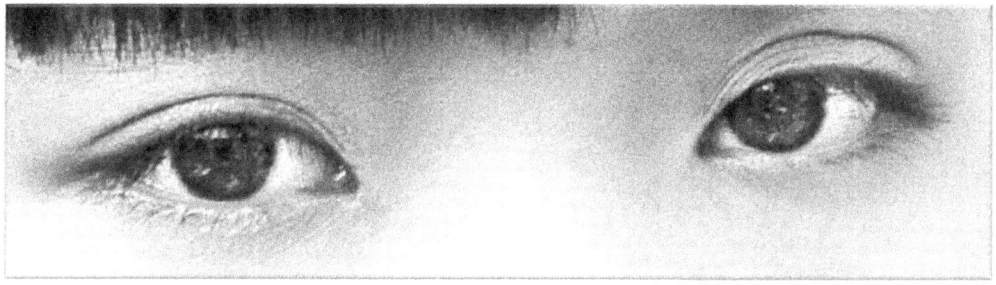

Figure 7-20

"Asian eyelid creases are quite different from the Caucasians' in terms of length, shape, and height." Chen (2000). As Dr. Chen notes, there can be considerable differences in eyelids that display the Epicanthic Fold. Figures 7-21 and 7-22 show two versions of a single lid, a female and a male.

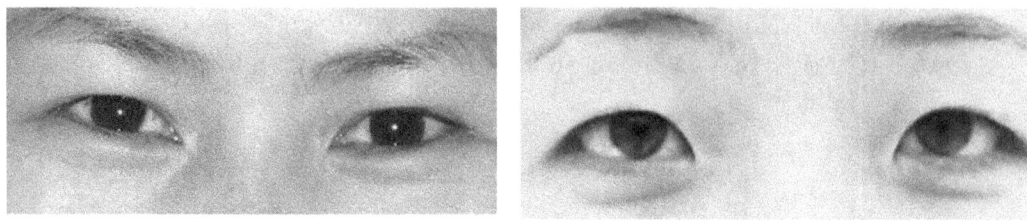

Figure 7-21   Figure 7-22

Individuals of Negroid descent also have more width between the eyes than Caucasians. The nasal bone is shallower than the Caucasian is but not as flat as Asians (Figure 7-23). The shape of the orbital cavity is square or rectangular. The eyes sit a few mm forward in the orbital cavity more than either Caucasians or Asians. You may also see the Epicanthic Fold in individuals of Negroid descent (Figure 24).

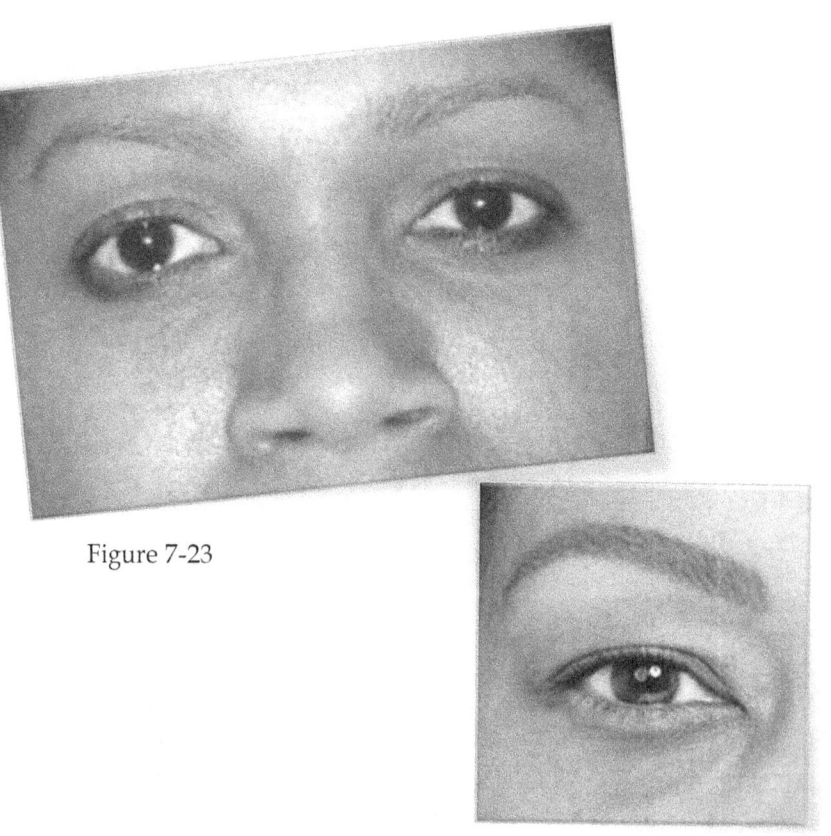

Figure 7-23

Figure 7-24

It is often hard for us to distinguish details on individuals of a race other than our own. We are used to seeing ourselves in the mirror and the majority of our relationships are usually with people of the same race. Our brain has formed a template for this look. If you are Caucasian and choose to sculpt an individual of Asian or Negroid descent, you will want to take several measurements prior to starting. These will include the length, and width of the eyelid, and the shape and width of the distinctive crease. These measurements are necessary to ensure the eyes are sculpted correctly. The same is true if you are of Asian or Negroid descent and plan to sculpt an individual of Caucasian descent. The details will be just as unfamiliar to you and require some preliminary study.

The Nose:

- *Schnoz*
- *Snout*
- *Beak*
- *Proboscis*
- *Honker*

He won by a nose. He's always nosing around. Keep your nose to the grindstone. Follow your Nose. It's no skin off my nose.

We could fill a page with the various synonyms for noses and the many ways we use the word as a verb. Unlike eyes and lips, however, there are no poems written to immortalize the nose. We're forever using these different expressions when we speak, but what can you say about the nose?

For starters, noses come in an endless variety of sizes and shapes. A cartooning book I have shows no less than 200 different ways to draw cartoon noses. Cartooning a feature, meaning to exaggerate the differences, is a good practice exercise. It forces you to study the shape to determine how it differs from the average. Regardless of how the nose appears on the outside, the internal structure is always the same. Simply put, the nose contains the nostrils, the organs of smell and functions as a passageway for air as we breathe.

The nasal bone itself begins between the orbital cavities and extends only a short distance. The rest of the length is **Cartilage**. Cartilage is a stiff, but flexible, connective tissue found in many areas in the body. It is stiffer than a muscle, yet not as hard and rigid as bone. This flexibility allows for the wide variety of noses we see every day.

On a face, the nose begins between the eyes. It widens out along the tent-shaped nasal bone and then tapers back in on the sides before it widens into the nostrils (Figure 7-25). Run your fingers down the sides of your nose to feel this indentation.

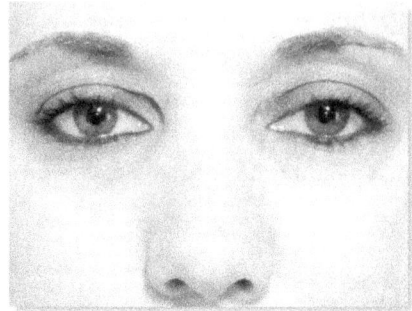

Figure 7-25

The angle of the Nasal Bone, the width of the Nasal Opening, and the length of the Nasal Spine are used together to reconstruct the nose. Still, the nose is one of the hardest parts to get right. Often the delicate bones of the nasal opening are broken or missing altogether. This leaves the artist with even more of a challenge in reconstructing the nose.

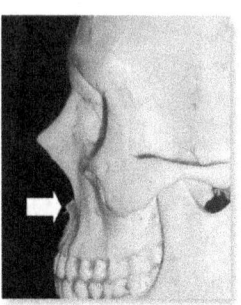

The **Nasal Bone** is a guideline for the forensic artist. The **Nasal Spine** helps determine the shape of the nose. It juts out from the base of the nasal cavity, and its purpose is to support the protruding nose. This cast of a Caucasian male (Figure 7-26) shows a defined Nasal Spine. It projects downward, suggesting a large nose.

Figure 7-26

Figure 7-27 is an example of a Nasal Spine that projects straight out, suggesting a nose with that same projection.

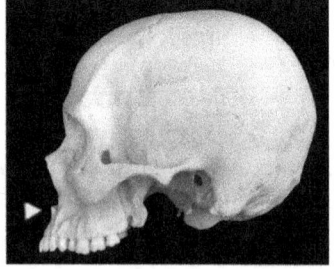

Figure 7-27

As you might expect, a short, upturned nasal spine would suggest a short, upturned nose - most likely on a female. The **Nasal Spine** also aids when assessing ancestry. It is prominent in Caucasians, less so in Asians, and small or absent altogether in Negroids. This results in the flatter and wider nose usually seen with African-Americans.

The visible nose consists of the **Nasal Bone**, the **Upper Cartilage**, **Lower Cartilage,** and the **Nostrils** (Figure 7-28). The **Upper Cartilage** is in one piece and fits horizontally below the nasal bone. The **Lower Cartilage** makes up the

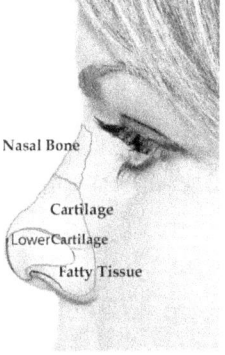

Figure 7-28

tip of the nose and is in two parts. You may even see an indentation at the tip of the nose where these two parts come together (Figure 7-28a). Gently rub your finger across the end of your own nose to feel the division of the two parts. The nostrils, on either side, are fatty tissue.

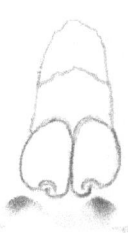

Figure 7-28a

If you have a bump on your nose, it most likely originates at the point where the nasal bone meets the upper cartilage. If these two are in line, the nose will be smooth. If not, you may see a "bump" on the exterior.

> **In facial reconstructions, when the "hits" are studied against a photograph of the victim, often the nose is the most "recognizable" feature.**

The shape of the lower cartilage determines if you have a little button nose or a large, bulbous one. A large nose with a hook results from a long nasal bone and a short nasal spine. Study noses in profile and make notes of the different shapes on males and females, older and younger individuals, as well as, different ethnicities. We might not consciously think about noses, but they play an important part in how we recognize others. When we see someone, the brain catalogues the individual characteristics. In a split second, it fits them together like a puzzle and sends the information to the part of the brain that allows us to recognize someone. How many times do you recognize a person in profile before you see them face to face? Each individual has a distinctive nose, and the differences aid our brain in recognition.

A rough determination for the size of the nose is to measure the width of the nasal opening and add the estimated width of the nostrils. For Caucasians, the average width of the nostrils is 5mm on each side. For Negroids, the average with is 8mm. There are no specific measurements for Asians so an average between Caucasians and Negroids is used.

When sculpting a portrait, you will have the advantage of being able to measure the nose and see the shape before you begin. However, knowing how the nasal bone and the cartilage form the base for the nose will help you sculpt realistic noses.

Shaped like a wedge, the nose is the high point on the face then sweeps back gradually to the cheeks. In fact, only half the nose projects out above the lips, the other half is set back on the cheeks along the upper mandible (Figure 7-29).

Without a model, you can look through magazines for pictures of noses. Fashion magazines are a good source of close up photographs of different noses. Make a note of the angle of the nose then check the tip. Also, note the size and shape of different nostrils. The septum connects the upper lip to the nose. The shape and angle of the septum are both important when sculpting noses.

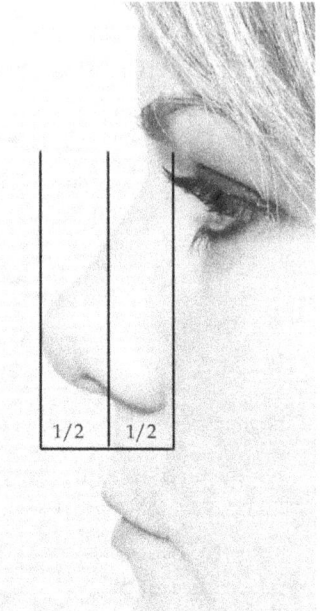

Figure 7-29

Differences in male and female profiles

- The **Glabella** in males has a sharper angle creating more of an indention at the top of the nose. Females have a softer curve.

- The male brow is more defined and projecting.

- The nose on a male tends to be somewhat larger, and more defined than the nose on a female.

- The male septum is straighter than that of a female. The female has a gentle curve.

- Male lips may be thinner but this is not always the case. They may appear so due to the larger amount of face area.

- Male chins are more pronounced and squarer than a female who usually has a rounded chin.

Add clay to the nasal cavity (Figure 7-30). You can use toothpicks to find the projection of the nose (Figure 7-31), note the tip slants backwards. Add small balls of clay for the nostrils (Figure 7-32). Figure 7-33 shows the nose further along.

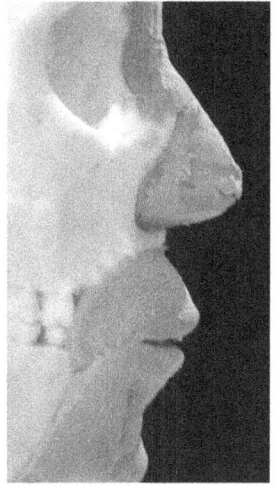

Figure 7-30

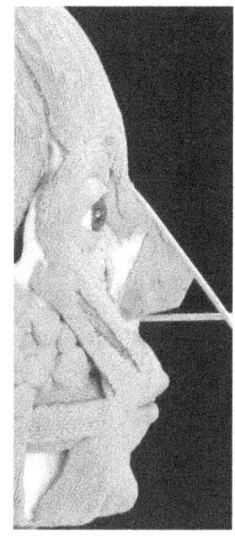

Figure 7-31

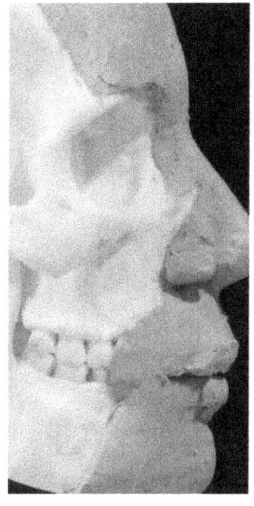

Figure 7-32

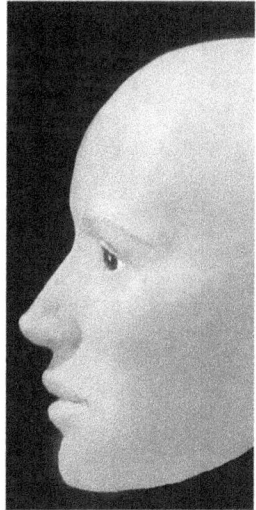

Figure 7-33

Figure 7-34 Noses:

African Derived Female and Male

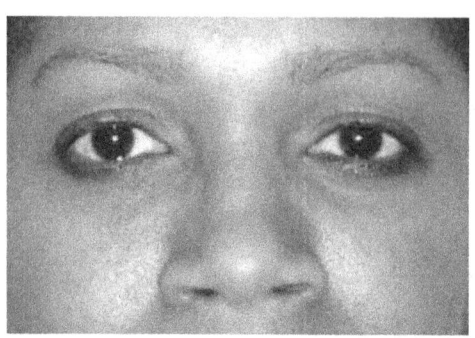 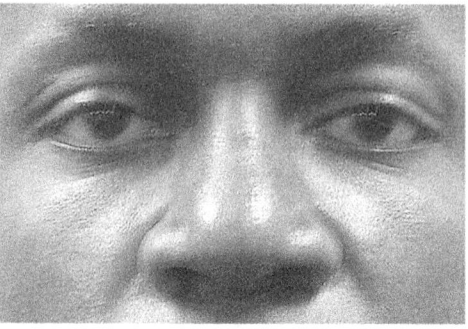

Asian Derived Female and Male

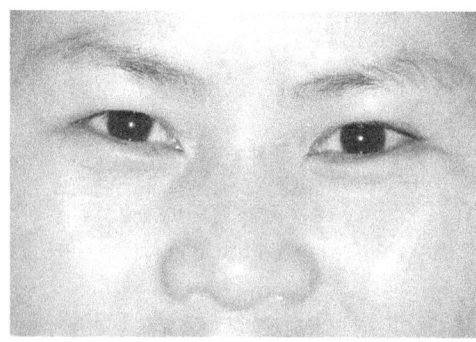 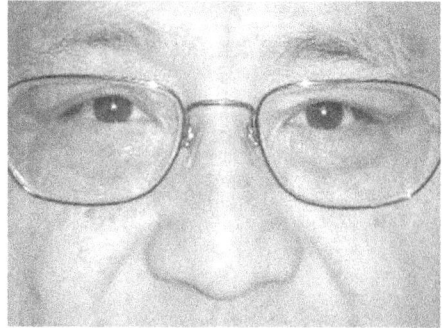

Caucasian Derived Female and Male

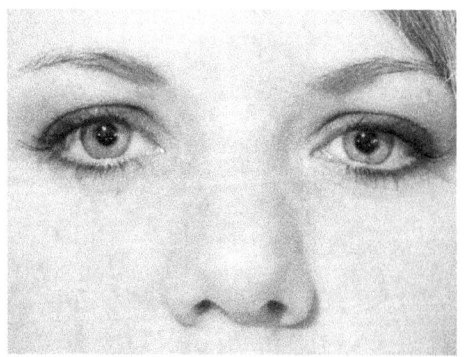 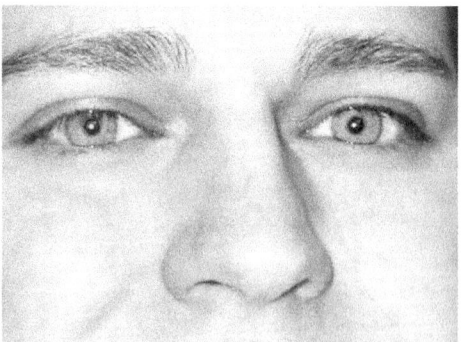

Sculpting details for realistic noses

- The **Nasal Bone**, or bridge of the nose, does not come straight down on the sides of the cheek. It widen out in a tent-like manner.

- The **Nasal Septum** divides the nose into two nasal cavities. The bottom of the septum connects the upper lip to the nose. There is a slight curve at the joining and it continues up between the nostrils.

- The **Alar,** the wings of the nose, form a C curve at the back of the nostrils called the **Alar Groove.**

- The nostrils may be a little lower or higher than the tip of the nose.

- The tip of the nose slants backwards and as we age, the tip of the nose tends to drop down.

- The **Philtrum** is the groove between the septum and the upper lip. The ridges on each side of the Philtrum line up with the peaks of the upper lip.

- There are no harsh angles on the face. The nose begins on the cheeks and projects forward. It doesn't sit on top of the face.

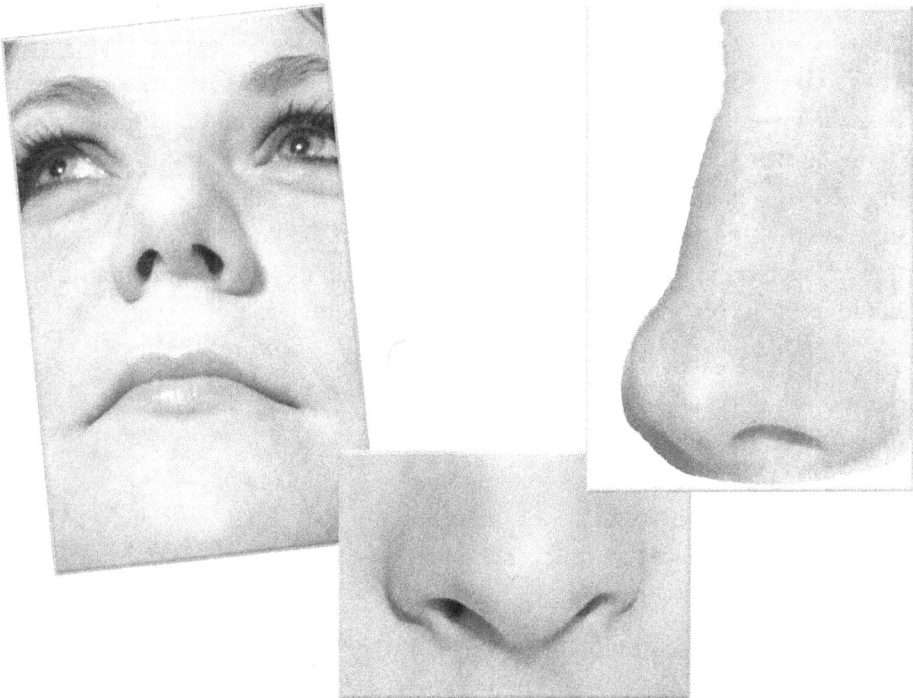

Figure 7-35

The Lips:

The eyes and nose must conform to the bony parts of the skull. The mouth, however, connected to so many other muscles becomes the most variable of the features. It freely changes form as you express different emotions. This allows you considerable latitude in sculpting.

From a visual perspective, the lips are second only to the eyes in the importance of features. They can be very expressive, sending a sweet and subtle message or a sensuous whisper. Like eyes, the lips are often the subject of poets. Writers portray them as luscious, pouting, and generous. On-the-other-hand, lips are also described as thin, cruel lines, depending on the character.

There are entire books written for romance writers that include lists of words and phrases to describe features. Her lips were full and rounded. Her generously curved and parted lips. The moistness of her full, red, mouth. These are just a few examples from *Romance Writer's Phrase Book,* Kent & Shelton (1984). The fact that there are books written about features emphasizes how important they are to a story and the word pictures are good for artists to keep in mind when sculpting.

You will remember from Part Five, The Muscles of Expression, that the smooth area we call the lips is only a portion of the entire lip area. Technically, the upper lip is the area between the nose, to <u>just above the lower edge of the upper teeth</u>. That sounds like a riddle. The result is that the upper lip is a mm or so thinner than the lower lip. However, that is such a tiny measurement that unless you are doing an actual reconstruction it's fine to use the halfway point as a dividing line. The lower lip is usually fuller and rounder than the upper lip. It extends down to the chin groove, the indentation between the lower lip and the chin. The lips connect to the cheeks at both sides. It may help to visualize the lips as having hinges at each corner, which allow them to open and close.

The smooth area is the **Vermillion.** The defining ridge you see around the lip rim on some individuals is the **Vermillion** Ridge (Figure 7-36). It is commonly associated with individuals of African descent but in all races the thicker the lips the more of a defining ridge you will see.

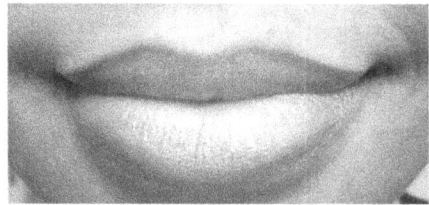

Figure 7-36

When you begin sculpting lips, consider the basic facts that will help you determine the size and shape. The differences in gender, as well as, the known differences of each ethnic group need to be considered. You might want to refer back to the section on bone structure to review the structure of the mouth. The shape and angle of the maxilla, mandible, and the teeth will help determine the final shape of the lips. When sculpting the mouth on a reconstruction the artist takes a few measurements prior to beginning. A general reference guideline for the thickness of the lips is the total height of the teeth, measured from the top of the upper teeth to the bottom of the lower teeth. A rule-of-thumb for the width of the mouth is for the corners to line up with the center of the eye on each side. Forensic artists may also use the position of individual teeth to help determine the width.

If you observe people with their mouth in a relaxed position, the lips are slightly parted, and the center four teeth are usually visible (Figure 7-37). This is often described as a seductive position. It is actually the result of the tiny piece of cartilage under the Knob of the Mandible. This slight separation ensures the teeth do not knock together.

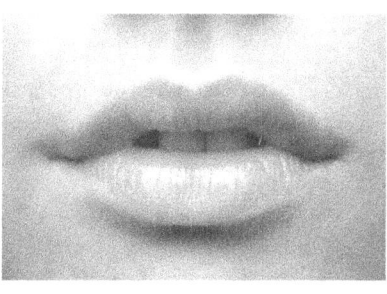

Figure 7-37

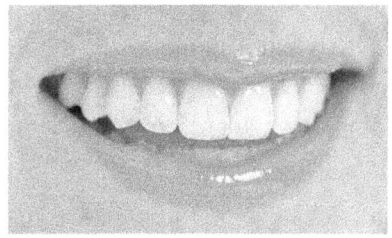

The bottom teeth are not usually visible unless the mouth is open in a wide smile (Figure 7-38).

Figure 7-38

Younger individuals often have a depression, or dimple, at the corners of the mouth (Figure 7-39).

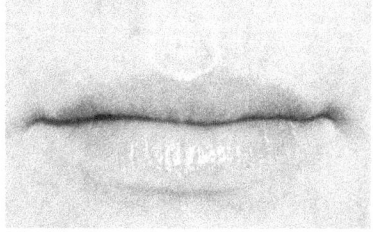

Figure 7-39

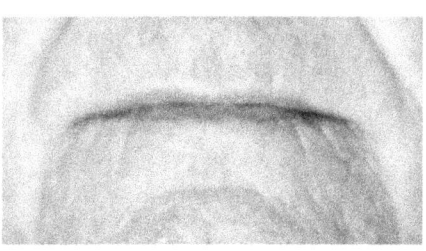

As individuals age, fat and tissue in the lips diminish. The lips thin and the upper lip drops below the dividing line of the teeth. In addition, as the muscles relax, the lips may appear to turn down at the corners (Figure 7-40).

Figure 7-40

There is an endless variety of lips. Study your own lips, those of your family and friends, and pictures in magazines to see the different shapes. Cosmetics often play a big part in the appearance of women's lips. Lip pencils and lip color can outline and reshape the lip area so they appear fuller, more rounded, and sculpted than they actually are.

Practice sculpting lips on a rounded surface, an empty jar is perfect to get the rounded conformation of the mandible and you can find them in any size.

Sculpting Details for Lips

- The corners of the lips pull back and around the curve of the mandible when smiling. It's only when you have a wide, open mouth laugh that the lower mandible drops down and back causing the lips to stretch and flatten.

- The peaks of the upper lip, line up with the outside ridges of the **Philtrum.**

- You can use a tool to incise a vermillion ridge right at the edge of the lips. For small figures, I prefer to only indicate this line.

- You can use a flat, semi-stiff brush to pull from the inside edge to the lip rim. Once smoothed off this leaves an edge without being obvious. If you lose the fullness while doing this, add clay back to reach the desired fullness.

- Some sculptors, such as Bruno Lucchesi, prefer to define lips with a line incised right at the edge so it will catch the light and highlight the lips. *Modeling The Head in Clay,* Bruno Lucchesi (1996).

It's a good idea to make several lip studies of different individuals to practice different techniques. Then decide which look you prefer for your own sculptures.

110

Once the clay is in place, use a sharp, flat tool to separate the lips (Figure 7-41).

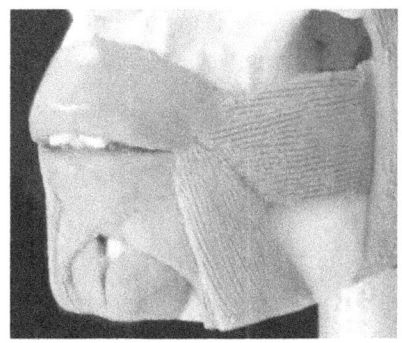

Figure 7-41

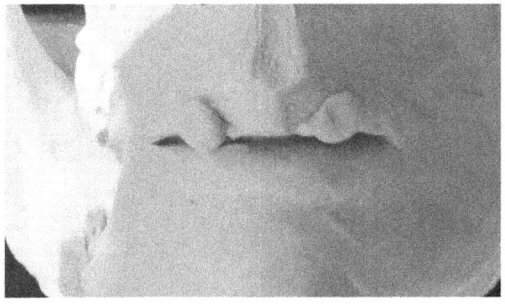

Figure 7-42

Use your finger or a tool to put in the **Philtrum** (Figure 7-42), the vertical groove between the upper lip and the nose. Pull it right down into the lip, which will give you the peaks of the upper lip. From the dividing line, push the upper lip up and the lower lip down. To add contour to the lips add three small balls of clay to the upper lip, one in the center, and one on either side.

Add two to the bottom lip, one on each side of the centerline (Figure 7-43). Use a tool to smooth and round the edges without losing the contours.

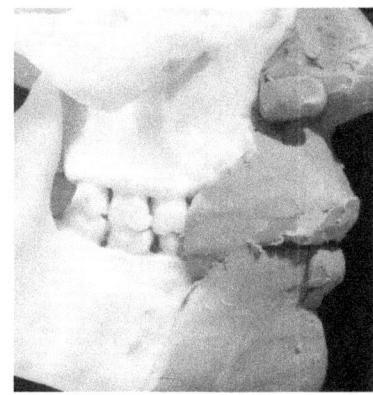

Figure 7-43

The Depressor Labii muscles are indicated by two small pieces of clay under the lower lip at the outer ends. This will also help support the lower lip while you're working.

Lips in Progress – Figure 7-44

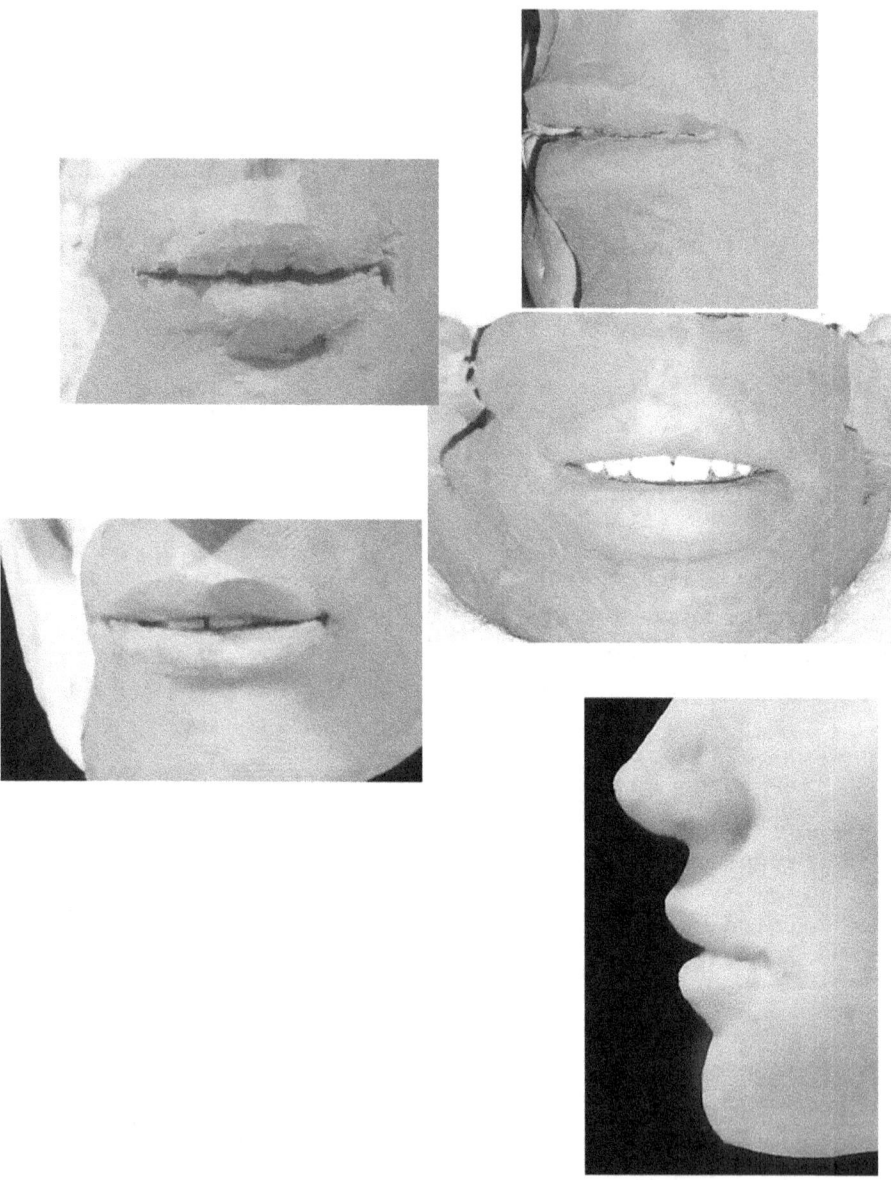

We tend to think of women's lips as full and rounded and men's lips as thin. In reality, men's lips are shaped the same. It's the addition of cosmetics that generally make the difference in how they appear.

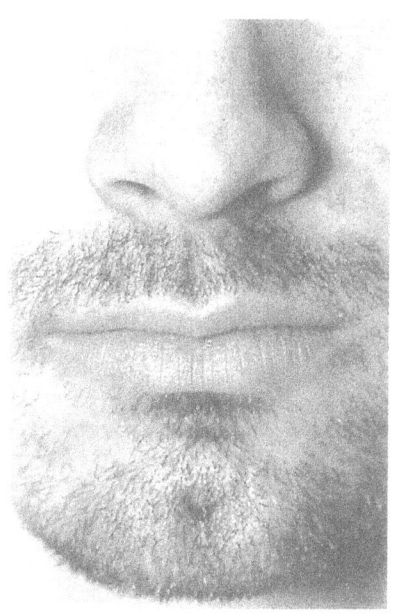

Facial hair on men grows in a specific pattern around the Vermillion (lips). A full mustache or beard may give a different impression but you can see how the growth of the hair follows the shape of the lips (Figure 7-45).

Figure 7-45

The Ears:

There are really no mysteries to sculpting the ear. In fact, I think you will enjoy it once you learn how simple they are to sculpt. As with all the features, the size and shape will differ from one person to another, but the basic anatomical form will stay the same.

Admittedly, ears are a funny shape. However, understanding why the ears have this specific conformation makes it easier to appreciate the form. The ridges and folds of the ear, plus the cupped shape, are ideally suited for collecting sound waves and directing them to the ear canal. You can help funnel more sound waves by cupping your hand behind your ear. Elderly people and those hard of hearing often do this without thinking. The different curves of the ear folds help the brain determine the direction of a sound. The ear points forward to better hear sounds coming from in front of you. Sound waves coming from behind you will bounce off the ear differently.

Ears are located on each side of the head. A "rule-of-thumb" is to draw a line top to bottom and front to back. Then place the ear at the intersection of the two lines. Once again, rules-of-thumb only work if the foundation of the head is correct.

One of the first things a beginning artist learns is that the head is "egg shaped". It is true that viewed straight on the shape does resemble an egg. Unfortunately, this often leads to making the entire head an egg shape. When sculpting, keep in mind **the distance from the front of the head to the back of the head is equal to the distance from the top of the head to the bottom.** There is a slight variance between Ethnic Groups, but not much. The Cranium rounds out at the back of the head to surround and protect the brain. It then curves back in, level with the base of the nose (Figure 7-46). Using an egg shape, you would need a second egg (cut in half), and the larger half added to the back of the head to get the correct profile.

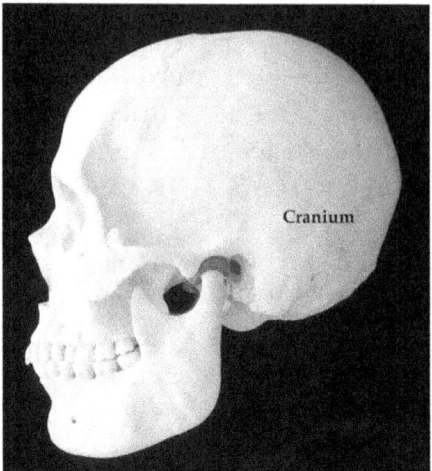

Figure 7-46

The ears are a vital part of our anatomy, and there is a very specific location to place them. Anatomically, they cannot be sited any other place. Once you learn how to locate the correct spot, you will always be able to situate the ears properly.

A simplified explanation for the location of the ears is the location of the **External Auditory Meatus** (Figure 7-47). This is the opening in the skull for the ear canal. The **Auricle**, the external portion we call the ear, serves as a receptor to funnel sound into the passageway. Sound waves, gathered from the environment around us, are channeled into the opening in the **Auricle**. They travel down the ear canal to the middle ear, which turns them into vibrations. The vibrations hit the eardrum and the brain interprets them as sounds we can understand.

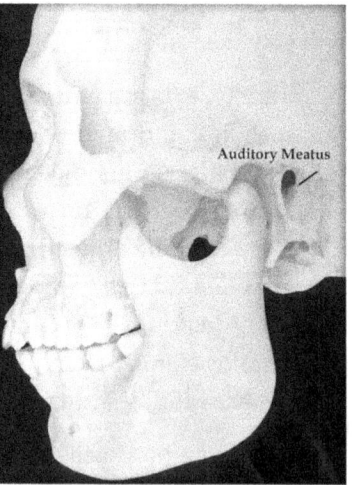

Figure 7-47

For us to hear sound, the external ear must be over the Auditory Meatus, the opening in the skull for the ear canal.

A guideline to locating the ear properly is the angle of the **Mandible**. This is easier to understand using your own jaw line. Beginning at the chin, trace your finger back to the angle of the **Mandible**. Continue up the back of the **Mandible** (the **Ramus**) to the ear and your finger will be right at the opening of your ear. This is where the **Auditory Meatus** is on the skull. When sculpting, remember to keep the ear behind the angle of the jaw (Figure 7-48).

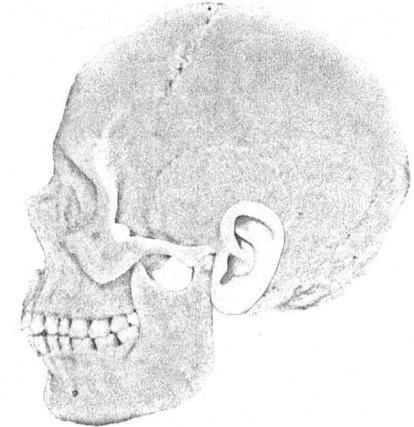

Figure 7-48

I suggest you make a study sample of ears, a left and a right, and keep them in front of you when you're sculpting. Oil-base clay is good to work with when practicing as it never hardens and is reusable. You can make the same ear over and over a hundred times till you have the perfect ear or make a line-up of different ears. Once you have the perfect ear, you can make a plaster cast to use as a study cast.

Plaster study casts of famous sculptures are available at art stores that carry sculpting supplies. Artists have used these for years. They are easy to make, however, and I recommend you make your own using one of the simple molding materials available in the crafts store. This way, you have your own work and can make sample ears for men, women, and children.

On small sculptures or Art Dolls, ears are often indicated, rather than sculpted. You might ask, if it isn't seen why go to all the work? Sculpting the details, even though they will not be seen or just partially seen, is a *WOW* factor for anyone viewing your work. When you have the ears fully sculpted, the hair takes on a more realistic shape and the ears might be seen peeking out between the strands, just as in real life. The fine details are what sets your work apart from others and appeals to collectors.

Even on a tiny fayrie creature, ears are important. They may be presented in unusual fayrie-like shapes, but they must still be anatomically correct. It should appear that the tiny person could hear raindrops falling and leaves rustling as she flies through the forest.

A rule-of-thumb is the ear will be the same length as the nose and about the same angle – or – about the same angle as the jaw. Another rule-of-thumb is that vertically, the ear should begin at the brow line and end level with the bottom of the nose. Although both of these are often true, you know from looking at the people around you that there are many individual differences. This is where Intelligent Observation and your sketching exercises pay off. Carry your sketchbook with you and when you have a few minutes, sketch what you see around you. It doesn't have to be perfect, just enough detail to give you a starting point back in the studio.

Ears attach smoothly in the front where they meet the cheeks. The lobe may hang completely free or be attached to the cheek. The ears angle away from the head in the back more than you might think they do. There is about a fingers width between the head and the outside rim of the ear (Figure 7-49). Go ahead and check your own ears.

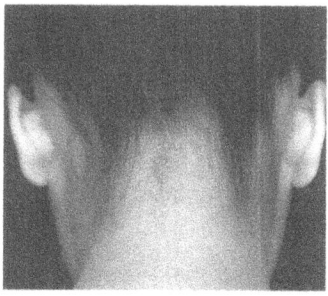

Figure 7-49

An easy mistake is to sculpt the ears too flat against the head. To avoid this you can make a platform for the ears to sit on. Form a ball of clay slightly smaller than your desired ear. Cut it in half and flatten one side with your thumb. This will give you a "C" shape, flat on one edge with a ridge on the other. Check that you have a right and a left side then position them in the correct spot for the ears.

Why is it so necessary to have the ears in a specific spot on the head? In addition to being anatomically correct, the ears help balance the head. If the ears are placed too far from the nose, the head will appear too thin and the back of the head too small. If the ears are placed too close to the nose, the front of the head will appear flat. If the ears are located too high, the lower portion of the face will seem too long. If too low, the opposite is true.

There are a couple of easy ways to build your ear. One is to roll a larger ball of clay than you did for the platform. Follow the same procedure, cut it in half, and slightly flatten both halves into a C shape (Figure 7-50). This gives you the depth to cut in the Concha and begin forming the ridges. Work with the entire thickness, removing clay and shaping the ridges as you go along (Figure 7-51). When you're satisfied, complete the shape of the outside rim, and use a scalpel to cut off any excess clay.

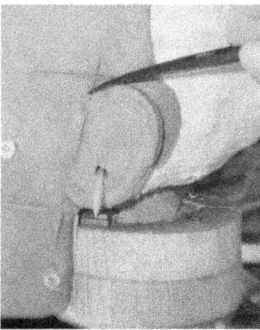 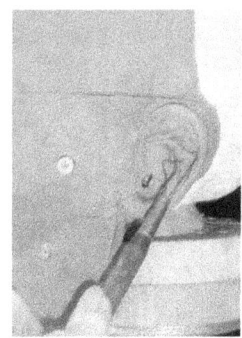

Figure 7-50   Figure 7-51

Another easy way is to begin with a rope of clay. Don't worry about the length as you will cut off any extra. Form the clay into a question mark (Figure 7-52). This gives you a starting point for the outside rim of the ear. Pull the clay to the inside and begin to form the ridges and valleys (Figure 7-53).

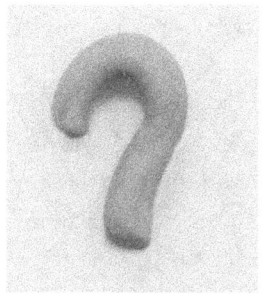 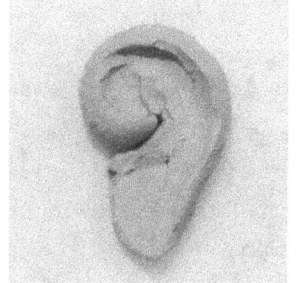

Figure 7-52   Figure 7-53

Study the details of the ear and the names of the individual parts (Figure 7-54). Some of the names will be easy to remember; a few you just have to memorize. It will not take long to become familiar with the names as you begin sculpting ears. If you remember the Tragus, you will remember the Anti-Tragus. The Helix is easy to remember as it forms a ridge around the edge of the ear, and the Antihelix forms the curving ridge in the center of the ear. You can use this diagram of an ear to sculpt a study ear with the correct anatomical details.

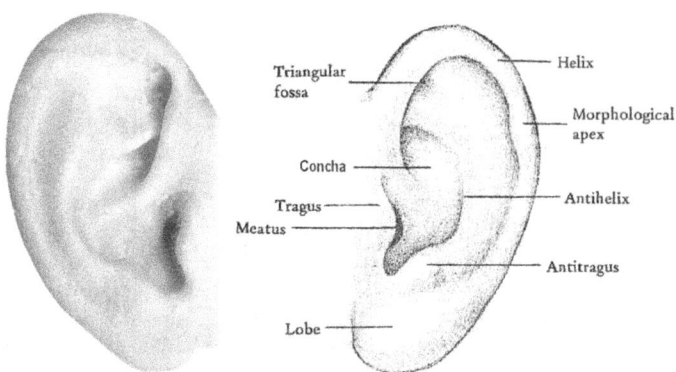

Figure 7-54

- A **Meatus** is an opening in the skull and the opening in the ear is the **Auditory Meatus**. This is the "hole" in our ear that allows sound waves to enter and fluids to drain out.
- The **Concha** in the center is shaped like a conch shell, easy to remember, right?
- The Morphological **Apex** is the peak - Apex meaning, "at the peak".
- **Fossa** is a Latin word for ditch, so the **Triangular Fossa** is a small triangle shaped "ditch" in the upper corner of the ear.
- A **Helix** is a circular or curving line; here the **Helix** is the outer ridge of the ear.
- The **Anti-Helix** is a curved ridge around the Concha.
- The **Lobe** is easy to remember, as we are already familiar with that name.
- The **Tragus** is the small tag of cartilage that projects over the opening of the ear as a form of protection.
- The **Antitragus** is a similar shaped projection on the opposite side. These form a U shape between them and together they protect the **Auditory Meatus**.

The ear is one of the last things you will add to the head. Complete the sculpting of the head and features, smooth the clay, and touch up any details.

Sculpt a basic ear and once you are satisfied with the shape, sculpt a second one. Before you apply them take a minute to compare the two ears. Verify they are of equal size and that you have a right and a left ear. By habit, we get so caught up in doing the same thing it's easy to forget the second ear has to be an opposite of the first. It's funny and frustrating when you proudly set your new ears in place and realize you've sculpted two right or two left ears.

Locate the **Auditory Meatus** and place your clay platform over the opening, keeping it behind the Mandible. Blend the edges into the clay at the back of the head. Place the ears on top of the platform and check front and back to make sure the distance from the head is equal on both sides (Figure 7-55). Continue shaping the ridges following the diagram in Figure 7-54. You will need small, rounded tools to shape the interior of the ear. Dip a q-tip in baby oil and run it around the interior to smooth any tool marks.

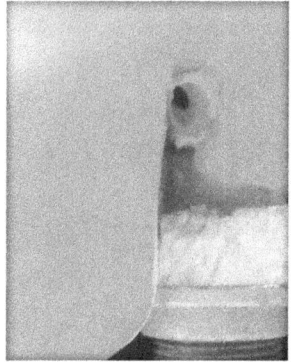 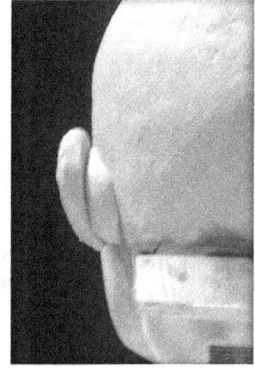 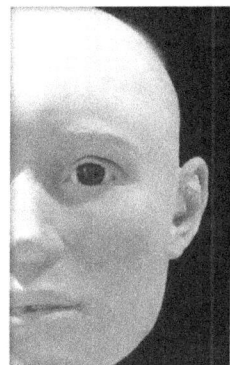

Figure 7-55

When you are satisfied with the contours, fill in the opening with clay and add the Tragus. This small piece of cartilage attaches smoothly to the cheek and extends over the opening in the ear to protect the ear canal (Figure 7-56).

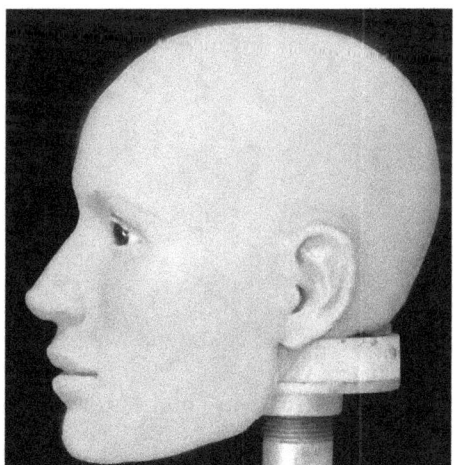

Figure 7-56

Ears come in all sizes and shapes and ear lobes may be attached or hang loose. Regardless of age or gender, the anatomical parts will be the same. Kayden isn't a year old yet but his ears are well developed.

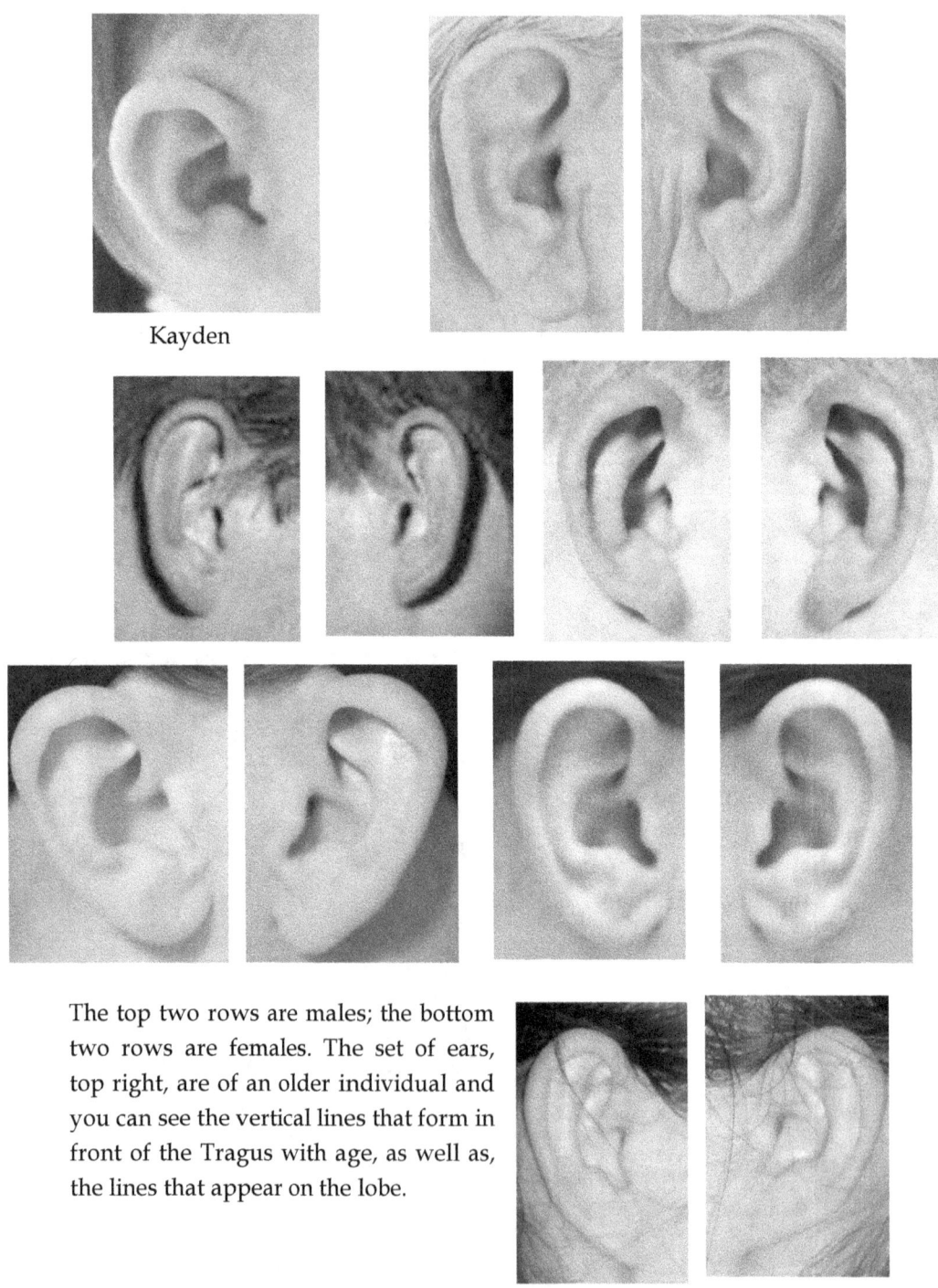

Kayden

The top two rows are males; the bottom two rows are females. The set of ears, top right, are of an older individual and you can see the vertical lines that form in front of the Tragus with age, as well as, the lines that appear on the lobe.

Part Eight

Expression Lines

Expression Lines

*I*t is commonly agreed among scientists that there are approximately seven facial expressions common to all societies. These basic expressions are inherent rather than learned. They are Happiness, Surprise, Fear, Anger, Contempt, Disgust, and Sadness. Psychologist, Paul Ekman, researched remote New Guinea tribesman who could neither read nor write, and who had never been exposed to the media. Yet the same universal expressions were observed.

Physiognomy, the theory that a person's physical appearance (especially the face), reveals deeper characteristics was of great interest to Aristotle (384-322 BC). In a discussion on the subject, he said "Everyone knows that grief involves a gloomy, and joy a cheerful countenance....there are characteristic facial expressions which are observed to accompany anger, fear, erotic excitement, and all the other passions."

Hundreds of years later, Charles Darwin wrote "…It has often struck me as a curious fact that so many shades of expression are instantly recognized without any conscious process of analysis on our part. No one, I believe, can clearly describe a sullen or sly expression. Yet many observers are unanimous that these expressions can be recognized in the various races of man." *The Expression of the Emotions In Man and Animals* (Darwin 1872).

More recently Gary Fagin has written "…the slightest suggestion of a smile can start a conversation between strangers; the slightest suggestion of a frown can start an argument between friends". He goes onto say, "…when we look closely at expressions like smiles and frowns, we realize how little on the face has to change for us to recognize an altered mood. When we draw an expression, we then realize that there is a gap between the recognition of an expression and the recreation of one." *Facial Expression* Fagin (1990).

You cannot deny that human emotions have an effect on facial expressions. It is easier to recognize an expression than it is to recreate it in sculpture. The particular expression you want can be elusive to capture. A slight widening of the eyes and lifting the eyebrows will be perceived differently depending on the situation. An unexpected check in the mail might cause you to lift your eyebrows and widen your eyes in pleasure. If it turns out to be an unexpected bill, you might use the same expression, but an observer would not see the same thing. You might have also used this expression to portray doubt. I call it the….are you sure you're telling the truth? Your child has just told an outrageous tale and you widen your eyes, lift your eyebrows, tilt your head down, and wait. Without me saying a word, my children would often respond, it's true Mom, I swear! Just before they smiled and said, just fooling. Very small changes in the lips can make a difference in appearance. A slight widening indicates the beginning of a smile. Rolling them in or pursing them, shows displeasure. Your knowledge of the actions involved in different expressions will make it easier to capture what you see. It is important to know the technical aspects of working with clay, as well as, the bone structure and muscle anatomy. Just as important, and maybe more so, is knowing how the features change as the expression changes. This is a more complex subject and involves an artistic proficiency to bring a sculpture to life.

We can borrow some tips from cartoonists who manage to portray emotions with simple lines. Follow these changes from normal to outright fright and you can see the eyes, brows and mouth all come into action. *Cartooning the head & Figure* (Hamm 1967).

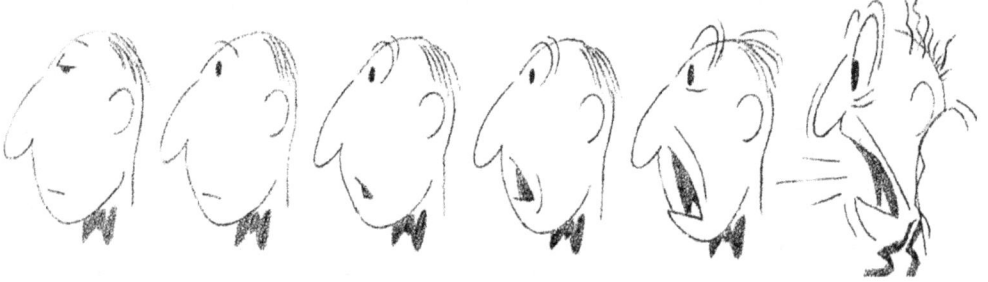

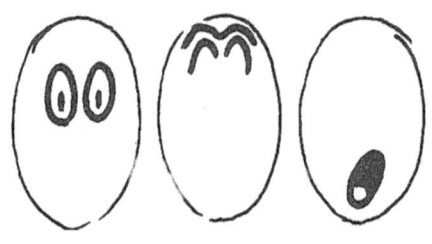

With only a few strokes of the pencil, cartoonists are able to portray recognizable expressions. Eyes open wide, the eyebrows lift, the forehead wrinkles, and the mouth drops open. You see surprise!

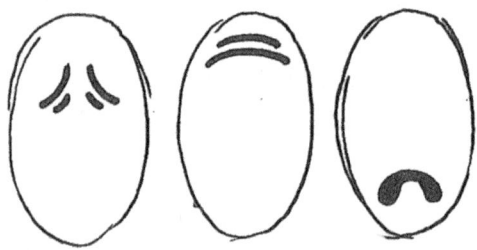

This time, the inside corners of the eyebrows brows pull in, and up. The eyes may be open or closed, the forehead wrinkles, and the mouth turns down at the corners. You see someone who is sad.

Each of these expressions involves the eyes, the eyebrows, and the mouth. Just a few changes in position and you create a new expression. Practice sketching simple expressions using just a few lines for each feature.

The next time you watch the news on television, watch the newscasters instead. In a span of a few moments, the newsperson might report on a tragedy, a happy reunion between family members, a political debate, and a segment on cute kittens and puppies. In the industry, they call it segueing, "To move smoothly and unhesitatingly from one state, condition, situation, or element to another". *American Heritage Dictionary 2009*. Television is a visual medium. They use facial expressions and body language to help convey the story they are reporting.

When the news comes on tonight, note their expressions as the camera zooms in and the broadcast begins. Watch the changes in their expressions as they move through the stories. It is politically correct to maintain an expression consistent with the story. However, they usually end the broadcast on an upbeat note. They reinforce the good feeling with a wide smile and friendly words to each other and to you, the audience. They want us to like them so "we'll see you right here at the same time, tomorrow night". Their ratings depend on you continuing to watch that channel. The same news is broadcast several times throughout the day. Turn the sound off once and "listen" to their facial expressions. My complaint with television is that it is a visual medium and you have to watch it to keep up with the story line, keeping you captive. Acting is another profession that relies on visual connection with the audience, through expression and body language. In the old silent movies, the actors used exaggerated expressions to convey the action on the screen without words.

As an infant, our expressions are spontaneous and involuntary. Before too many years have passed, though, we learn to school our expression to fit the occasion. You receive a gift you didn't want, but you are taught to smile and thank the giver. A co-worker says something that angers you, but you don't show it at the time. In these and other instances, we voluntarily display an expression that doesn't fit our emotions, but the muscles are still working.

Look in a mirror when you are on the phone. You will find your expression is mirroring the expressions in your voice, even though the other person can't see you. When you laugh and talk to your friends on the phone, your face will reflect happiness. A call to a repairperson may result in a neutral expression or even show irritation. Businesses often use this technique to train employees so the customer calling hears a pleasant friendly voice.

Most artists sculpt portraits with a serious or pleasant expression. You rarely see one with a wide smile. Changes in the mouth area can affect the entire face, the eyes, nose cheeks, and lips. A guffaw can actually distort the face. We don't see the changes as we are usually caught up in the laughter at that moment ourselves. It is easier for the individual viewing a portrait to visualize that person smiling than to see it frozen in time.

Earlier, you studied the muscles used to produce expressions, but how do you know how much effort produces the desired result? If you want to sculpt a particular expression, you can get some basic information by studying the changes in your own face. Practice in front of a mirror and observe others in different situations. Facial structure, weight, and age will have an effect on the appearance of each individual, but the muscles used remain the same.

When you are happy, the lips stretch back into a smile and form the beginning of a cheek bulge. As the smile widens into laughter, the lips are pulled further back, smile lines form from the nostrils to the mouth, and the cheeks press up against the lower lid narrowing the eyes. The lower jaw drops down, the upper lip thins, and six, to eight teeth, are exposed. The lower lip is stretched tighter than the upper lip, as it has to stretch around the curve of the lower teeth and then back up at the corners to meet the upper lip. With heavier individuals, the cheek bulge will be bigger to accommodate the extra layer of fat tissue. It will sometimes narrow the eyes to the point they appear closed. The skull has not changed, nor has the action of the muscle. The amount of fat and fluids in the tissues makes it look different.

How does this review of expressions tie in with expression lines? Read back over the preceding pages. Think about how many times a day you make a particular expression. You smile, you laugh, you frown, and you pucker your lips. Pick just one expression to use in this exercise. You probably smile several times in the morning as you greet your family, your co-workers, or strangers on the street. I'll pick 10 smiles each morning as an average figure. At lunchtime, you may meet a friend, fix lunch for your family, or do some shopping or run errands. Let's add another 10 smiles here. As you go through the afternoon and evening right up to bedtime, you probably smile another 10 to 20 times. Some smiles may be outright laughter while others may be as simple as just lifting one corner of the lip. However, every time, you used the same muscles.

Now, let's do the math. Ten smiles in the morning add another 10 at noon and 20 more before bedtime. This equals 40 smiles a day, multiplied by seven days a week, four weeks in a month, 12 months in a year. Or, an easier way to put it is 40 smiles a day multiplied by 365 days in a year. My calculations show that to be 14,600 smiles every year. Carried out even further – every ten years of your life you can expect to smile 146,000 times.

The Risorius muscle, nicknamed the "smiling muscle", has contracted, and relaxed more times than we can count. Have you ever had an elastic waistband that has stretched over time and now your pants don't fit as well? That's what happens to the Risorius muscle and all the other muscles in our face that we use every day to create various expressions. Over time, they begin to stretch, lose their elasticity and tone, and just like your pants, the skin begins to sag.

When your skin is young, thick, and full of elasticity, it can resist the muscle tension and the pull of gravity. When you stretch your lips into a smile, they bounce back smooth as ever. The skin does not develop a crease each time you smile, frown, or squint. However, as you age and the skin becomes thinner, drier, and less resilient. It begins to adhere to the underlying muscle tissue. Now when you smile or frown, the skin is pulled along with the muscle eventually creating a line that deepens into a crease or a fold.

There are actually three different types of wrinkles. Fine lines that are due to gradual loss of elasticity, expression lines appear where the muscles of facial expression cause permanent creases, and those that form as a result of gravity.

"The features of our face are hardly more than gestures which force of habit made permanent." This quote by Proust (1871-1922), is a very fitting way to describe the lines created by repeated facial expressions.

Here is a quick check of some everyday expressions. An inexpensive stand up mirror is good to keep in your work area to check out an expression on your own face when you're sculpting. This interactive website shows the facial muscles in action, which helps imprint the action in our brain. You can access this website by going to: http://www.artnatomia.net/index.html

Happiness: When we're happy, we smile. The corners of the lips draw back and may curve up a little. With a wide smile, the lips part and the upper teeth are visible. Wrinkles appear at the outer corners of the eyes, and the eyes narrow from the cheeks pushing up.

Surprise: The eyebrows lift causing horizontal lines to appear on the forehead. Eyes widen, stretching the skin around the eyes. The mouth opens and the jaw drops down.

Fear: When faced with something fearful, the eyebrows go up quickly and draw towards the center. Horizontal wrinkles may appear across the forehead with vertical lines between the eyebrows. The eye open wide showing the whites of the eyes. The facial muscles under the eyes get tense, the mouth opens, and the lips draw back into a rectangular shape.

Anger: Anger causes us to pull the eyebrows down creating vertical wrinkles between the eyebrows. We tighten our eyes and create lines in the eyelid at the corner and under the eye. We lift and flare the nostrils. All of these lines become more pronounced as our anger increases. Give yourself an intense, angry look in the mirror. Almost every muscle is tightened.

Disgust: When we are disgusted by something, the eyebrows lower. The upper lip is raised and the lower lip turns down. The nostrils lift, the nose wrinkles, and the cheek muscles tighten causing lines under the eyes.

Sadness: The inner corners of the eyebrows pull up creating vertical wrinkles between them. The corners of the mouth turn down. The lips may quiver and the eyes shed tears.

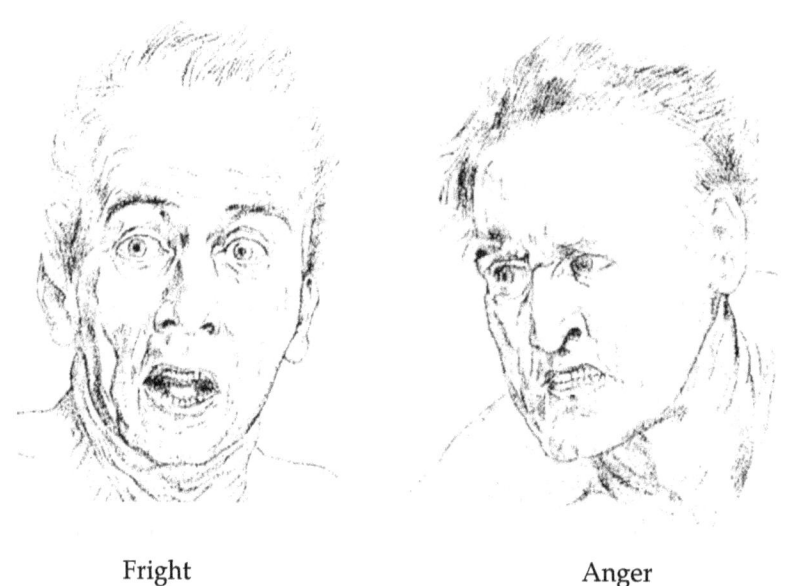

Fright   Anger

Part Nine

The Aging Process

The Aging Process

*A*ge, and how we show our age, is often a delicate topic. We are used to the face we see in the mirror every day so it is easy to continue to see ourselves as we once were. Aging is more a process of the body than the mind – they say you are only as old as you feel – so if you feel young that positive outlook will be reflected in your face.

When sculpting a figure, you have the freedom to portray them any way you like. For a realistic appearance, however, you need to keep in mind the changes that occur naturally and at what age. There can also be times in life, where the circumstances of the physical surroundings will have an effect on the outer appearance. Your priority as an artist is to keep the sculpture, and the setting, in perspective. For a forensic artist, it is important to be aware of when and how the signs of aging begin to appear. Age, health, and living conditions, if known, are all taken into consideration before beginning a reconstruction.

Each culture has certain characteristics inherent with their ethnic backgrounds. These genetic factors play an important role in how tough our skin is and how vulnerable to the sun, which is one of the primary causes of skin damage. Europeans, Scandinavians, Asians, Africans, and Hispanics tend to age differently and along different time lines.

Northern Europeans tend to have fair complexions and are more vulnerable to the sun. They begin to show signs of age earlier than those with darker skin do. Southern Europeans will have more olive skin tones. Asians have a yellow skin tone. Africans and African-Americans have a darker skin ranging from brown to almost black, which is less susceptible to the UV rays of the sun. The result is that Africans, African-Americans, and Asians do not show signs of aging until later in life and there is very little, if any, fine wrinkling of the skin till late in life.

With cosmetic surgery being within easy reach and the array of cosmetics available, women can appear to be younger, longer. However, time catches up with everyone and even the wealthiest, most glamorous of superstars will eventually show the effects of age.

The upper portion of the face is the first place we notice signs of aging. Laughter may be the best medicine for us, but not so for the skin around the eyes. Don't let this discourage you from laughing though! Even the act of closing our eyes creates wrinkles that are pressed into our skin as we sleep. You can feel on your own face that the bones around the eyes are much closer to the surface of the skin than in your cheek area. Without a layer of fat tissue, the skin will show lines and wrinkles sooner.

Collagen and elastin are both fibrous proteins that help make up the connective tissue in the skin. As the years pass, the production of collagen diminishes. The skin loses its elasticity and fatty tissue disappears. General health and living conditions, as well as, stress all play a part in how individuals age. There are some predictable changes, however, that occur in everyone around the same age in life. Keep in mind, we not only develop more lines as we age but the ones we have, become deeper and more pronounced. Stress, illness, and weight gain or loss, can have a negative effect on the skin. Three factors determine how your skin ages. They are age, genetics, and lifestyle.

At 18 years old, our skin is fresh, smooth, and firm. In the late teens the external shape of the face may still be developing. Males may take a few more years to mature as the mandible lengthens and broadens.

As early as the 20's though, you may begin to see lines developing. Crow's feet, 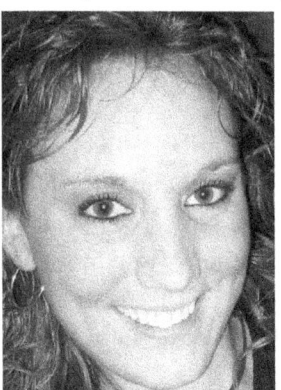 those fine lines radiating out from the corner of the eye, appear early. Fine lines may also appear under the eyes. These are associated with happy people who smile frequently or those who spend a lot of time outside and squint against the sun (Figure 9-1). At this point, women can hide these with cosmetics. Fine, horizontal lines across the forehead may also appear now. My husband has had one horizontal crease across his forehead since his early 20's, which has deepened into a groove over the years.

Figure 9-1

The number of facial muscles is, in part, the reason for the appearance of these early lines. Young people, especially, have very mobile faces. The different emotions that cross their faces daily means the muscles are working all the time. As the muscle contracts, it scrunches the skin into folds and wrinkles appear perpendicular to the muscle. The repeated actions of the same muscles in this delicate area cause fine lines to appear early at the skin folds.

The Frontalis muscle in the forehead is the vertical muscle between the eyebrows and the hairline. Its purpose is to raise the eyebrows. Think how many times every day you raise your eyebrows, frown, or wrinkle your nose. These are just a few of the actions that use the Frontalis and the Corrugator muscles around the eyes.

Within a few years, fine vertical lines begin to appear between the eyebrows and later, horizontal lines appear across the top of the nose. The muscles in this area get a lot of use, although most of the time, we are not even aware of the changes in our expression. In the 30's these fine lines become more noticeable. This is also when women begin to notice changes in their skin. It may be drier, not quite as smooth, or firm. Repeated sun exposure might have caused some pigment changes. Women may also begin to notice horizontal lines on their neck now.

On the lower part of the face, the Nasolabial crease will begin to deepen. The Nasolabial crease is the curved line between the nose and mouth that appears when you smile. This crease is seen in infants and other than deepening, it stays much the same over the years.

In the 40's, lines that were only slightly noticeable in the 30's, now deepen into actual wrinkles The forehead creases deepen and horizontal lines appear above each eyebrow continuing out to the temples (Figure 9-2). The skin of the upper eyelid may begin to relax, partially covering the eyelid crease. Lines under the eyes are a natural trait in some people. In others, lines under the eyes may be a result of sun damage, rubbing the area frequently or even an excess of fat in this area. Conversely, this area under the eyes can hollow out along the tear trough, causing you to look older than you are.

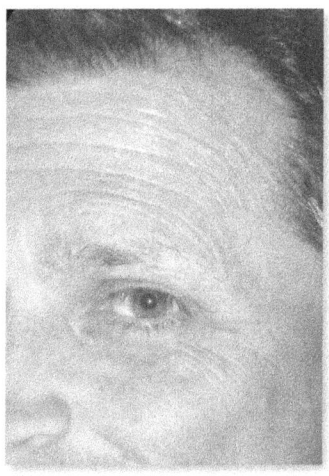

Figure 9-2

Women may see some thinning of the lips now and the beginning of vertical lines, radiating out from the lips. The horizontal creases on the neck may begin to droop. For men and women both, it is easier to gain weight now and harder to lose it. With weight gain, the jaw line will soften and the furrows in the cheek will deepen with the excess tissue.

The thinning and gradual loss of hair can make a dramatic change in the appearance of many men. Hair loss at the front gives men a receding hairline. However, the forehead creases will never be higher than the original hairline. That is where the Frontalis muscle ends. Women may also experience some thinning of the hair, although they have more options to disguise it with color and different styles.

The 50's are a time when definite changes are seen in most people. The entire face may appear to soften and lose its firmness. Excess weight may have caused stretching of the skin, which now sags. The forehead creases extend out to the temples and fine lines from the eyes can even cross over them. Forehead creases deepen approximately .5mm with each decade. At 40, the forehead creases will be about 1mm deep. By 60, they will have deepened to 2mm.

The Nasolabial crease may have become a fold now with the addition of more weight. Cheek wrinkles might line up outside the Nasolabial fold when you smile. The Buccolabial fold forms at the corners of the mouth. The Mentolabial fold or the chin groove deepens (Figure 9-3).

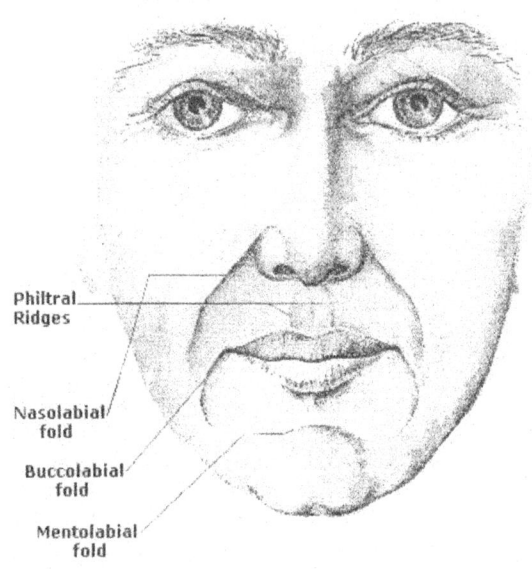

Philtral Ridges

Nasolabial fold

Buccolabial fold

Mentolabial fold

Figure 9-3

Entering the 60's individuals may show signs of aging differently depending on their lifestyle and exposure to the sun. The eyebrows and eyelids droop lower. As the skin relaxes, the facial lines begin to curve downward. The lines under the eyes curve down at the outer corners. When smiling several smile creases form behind the Nasolabial fold (Figure 9-4) often giving the impression that the lines at the outer corners of the eyes continue down to the jaw line.

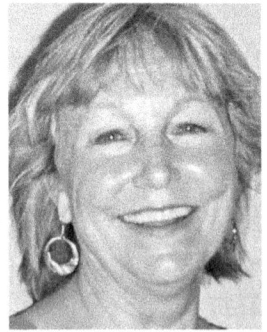

Figure 9-4

134

This is also the time many individuals develop fat pads under the eyes forming bags (Figure 9-5), or the "tear trough" may deepen forming hollows. Lines may extend out from the eyes curving down the cheek.

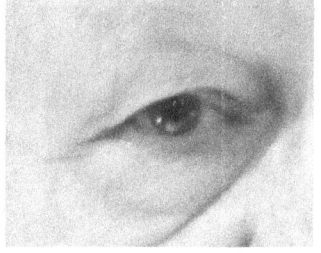

Figure 9-5

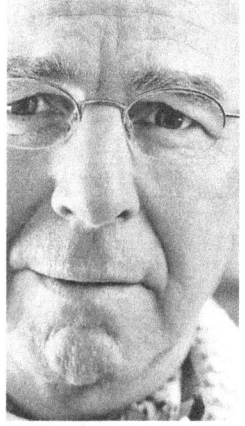

The Nasolabial and Buccolabial folds deepen and extend further down. As the cheeks lose their firmness, gravity takes over and the flesh sags, causing droopy jowls (Figure 9-6). Excess weight may form a double or triple chin but the definition of the Mentalis muscle, the chin, is still discernable. At the other extreme, the excess skin on the necks of thin individuals may form a Turkey Wattle.

Figure 9-6

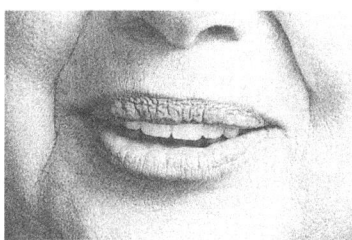

By the 60's most women's lips have lost their fullness and vertical lip lines, especially in women who have smoked, become more pronounced (Figure 9-7). Some women develop a horizontal line across the top lip, under the nose.

Figure 9-7

In the 70's men may continue to experience hair loss (Figure 9-8). Ears, like the tip of the nose, are made up of cartilage. With age and gravity, the ear lobes stretch and sag down.

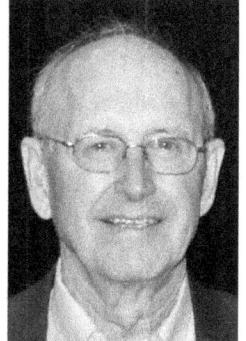

Figure 9-8

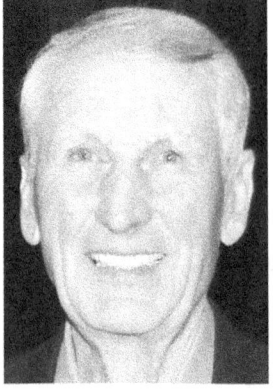

In men and women both, the tip of the nose drops down appearing to be longer than it was originally. The area in front of the ears, just in front of the Tragus, will develop vertical lines, as will the ear lobes on both men and women. Men especially may develop a long crease from the eyes to the jaw line (Figure 9-9). Excess hair on the eyebrows as well as in the nose and ears is more noticeable on men, although women can experience this also.

Figure 9-9

Creases continue to deepen; fine lines develop, crossing haphazardly in many directions across the skin. At this time of life, a little weight will soften the lines and fill in some of the creases (Figure 9-10).

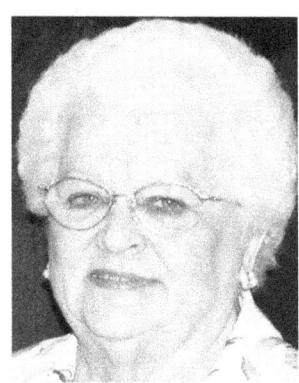

Figure 9-10

Study the pattern of lines and wrinkles on older individuals before attempting to sculpt them. Lines and skin folds follow definite patterns, varying slightly depending on the individual and their lifestyle (Figures 9-11, 9-12, and 9-13).

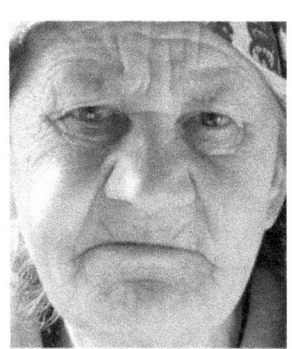

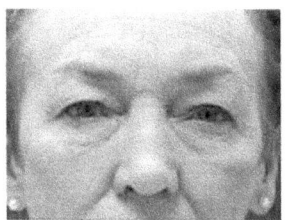

Figure 9-12

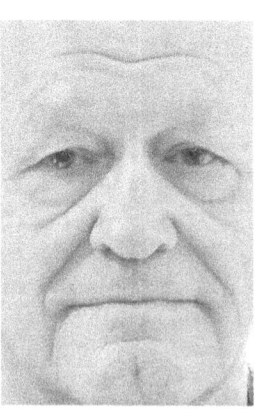

Figure 9-11

Figure 9-13

As a person reaches the 80's and even the 90's, the layer of fat under the skin thins out more and the excess skin lays in folds. Loss of teeth will cause the lips to thin even more and roll inward.

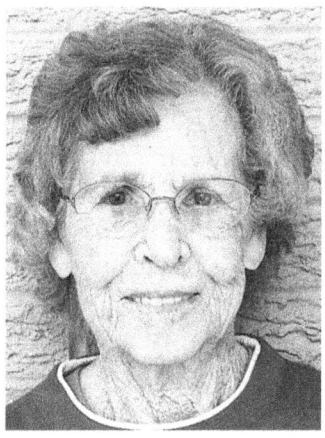
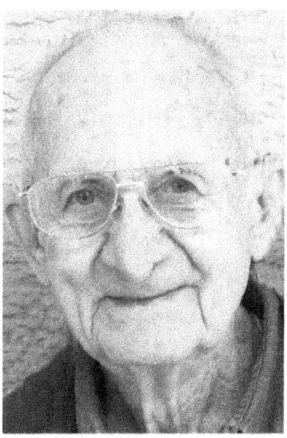

Each of these individuals pictured here have lived many years and the passage of time shows on their faces. However, their smiles and joyful expressions reflect a life well lived.

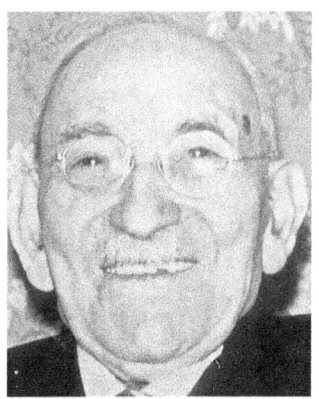
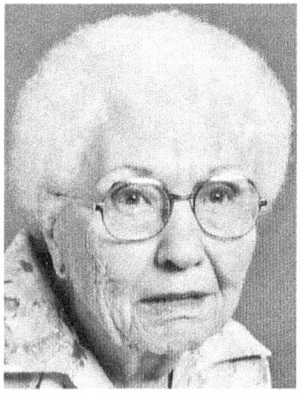
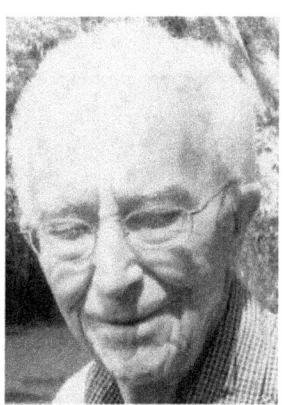

If you have the opportunity to compare photographs of family members at the same age you will have the best chance of seeing the resemblance over the years. A daughter may look more like her Father, and sons may closely resemble their Mother. Children often resemble one parent more at different stages in life. Still, in comparing photographs, you will usually see distinctive characteristics.

This is my Mother as a young woman and about age 44. I've always looked like my Dad, while my sister has always looked like our Mother. Yet today, people seeing us together comment on how much we look alike.

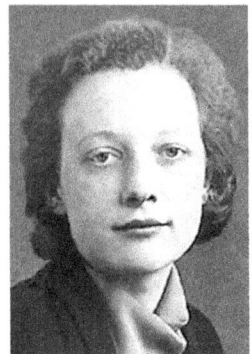
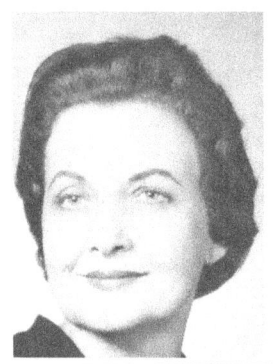
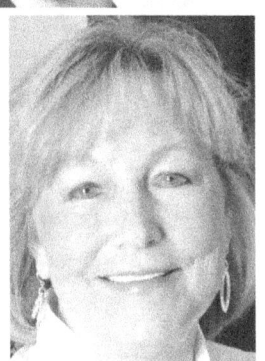
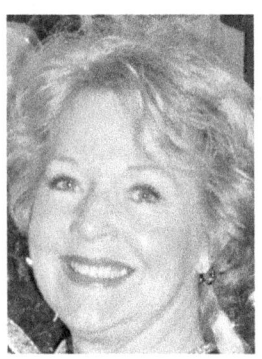

My friend Lisa VerPloeg, center, her Mother and oldest daughter.

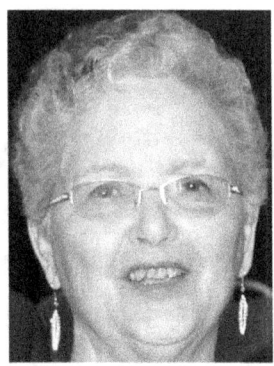
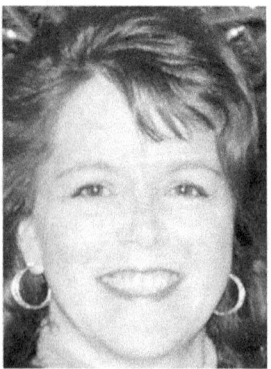
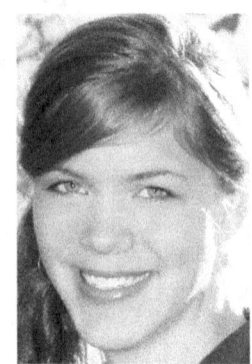

At first glance, you may not see much of a resemblance between the boys and the adults, because of the difference in ages. If you look closely, however, you can see a glimpse of what the boys will look like in the years to come. Shown here are three generations of VerPloeg men.

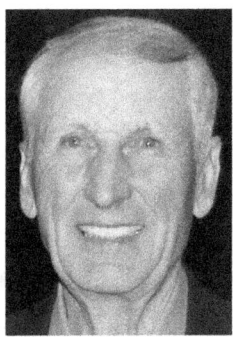 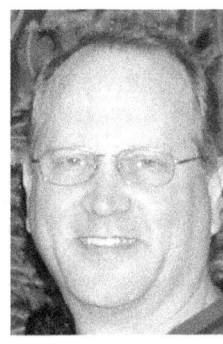 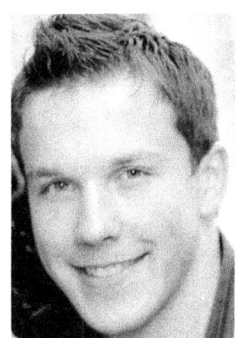

Below, are six generations of Floods beginning with my husband's great-grandfather, top left, and our youngest grandson, Ryan Flood, bottom right.

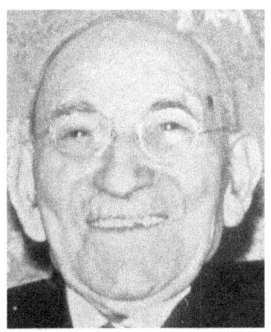 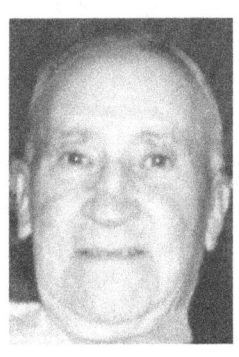 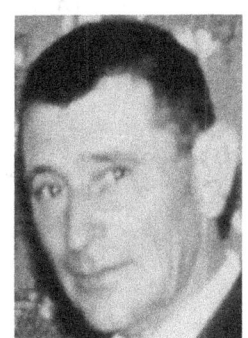

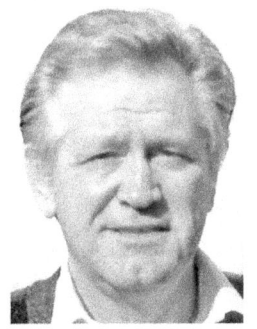 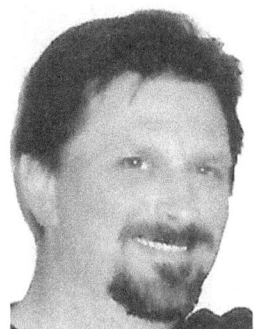 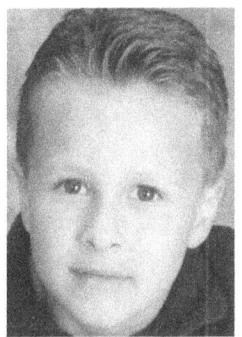

Age Progression: Birth to age 73. The dimple in the chin has remained constant throughout the years, and has been passed down to the following generations.

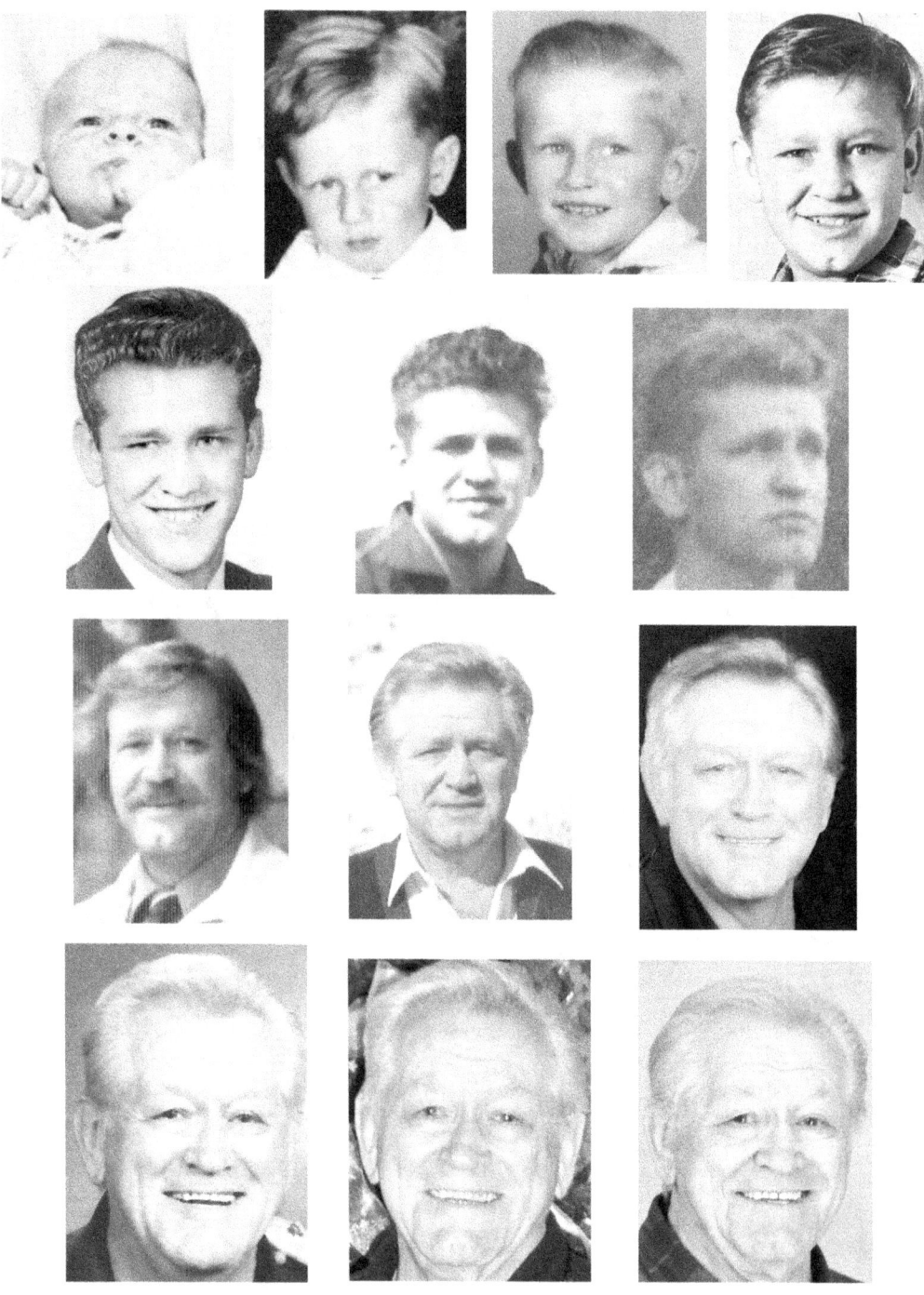

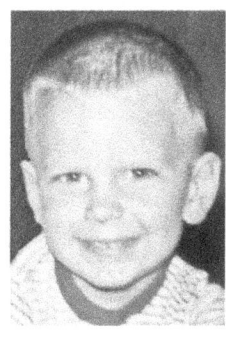
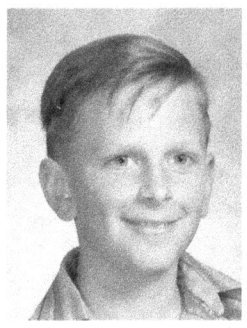
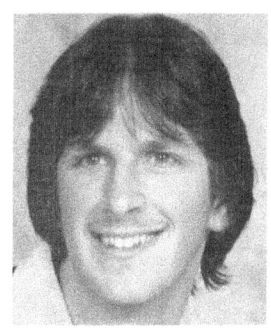

Harold

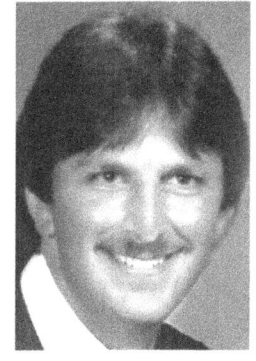
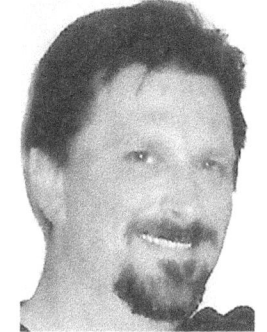
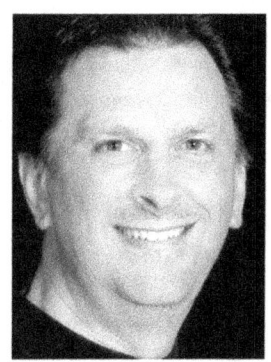

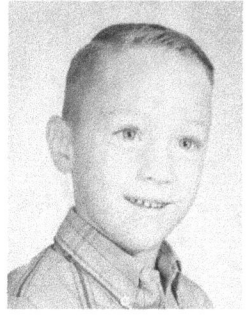
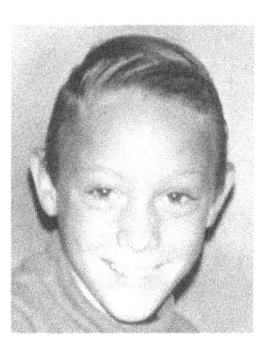
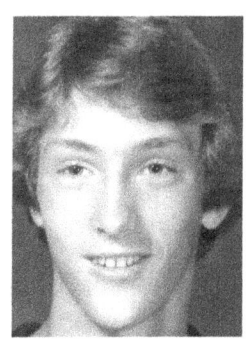

Bill

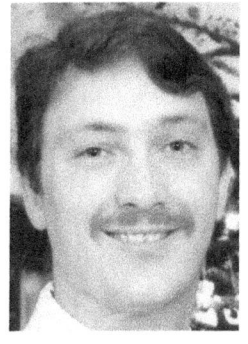
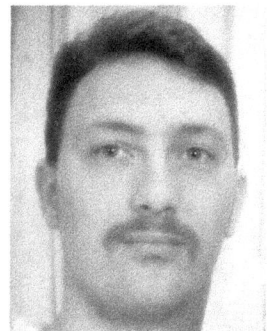
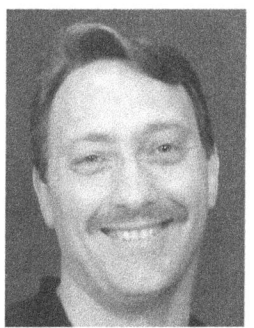

David,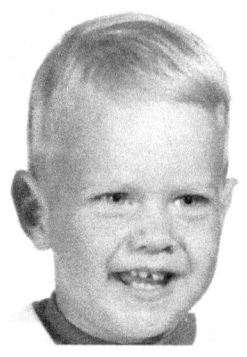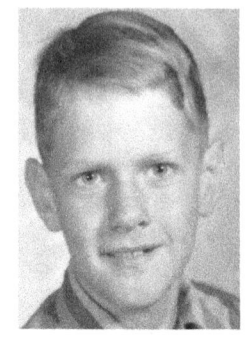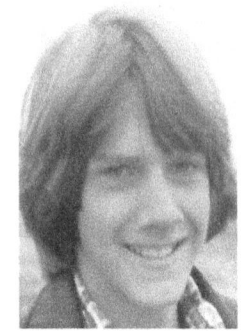

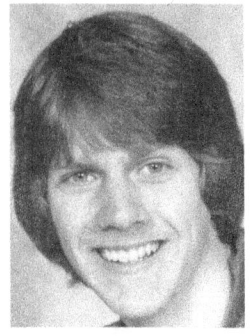 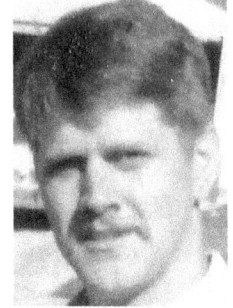 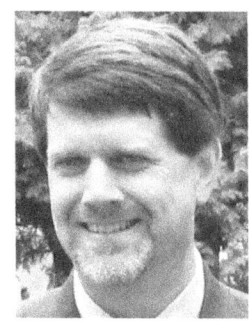

and his boys, our oldest grandsons.

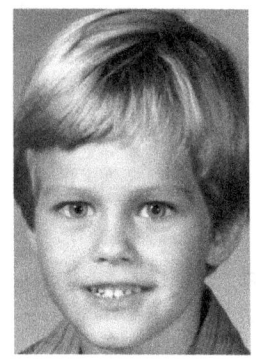 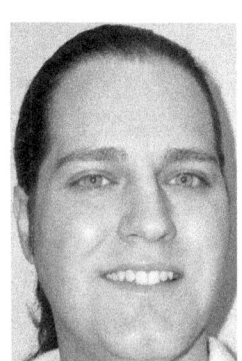

Michael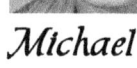

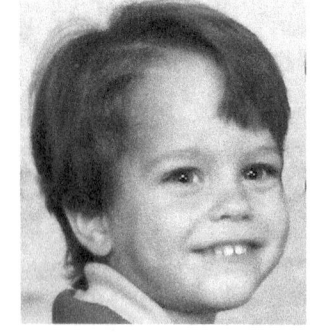 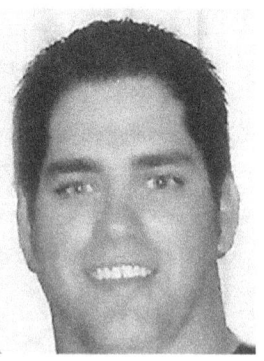

Christopher

142

Part Ten

Tools and Stands

Tools and Stands

Tools

Basic sculpting tools are all you need to begin with. If you're like me, over the years you've picked up one or two, here and there. Some become part of your everyday tools and you keep them forever, others get pushed to the back of the drawer. Here are a few I've accumulated over the years, some used for sculpting with earth clay and some that were originally used in making plaster molds. There are a few I wouldn't part with and others that are nice to have. You can obtain similar tools at art stores, the plaster tools are usually found through on-line art suppliers. I suggest you begin with the basic tools and add to your collection as you need them.

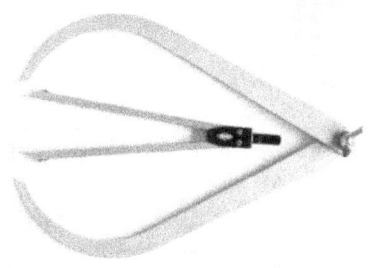

Spreading Calipers come in a variety of large and small sizes, as well as different shapes. They are used for exterior and interior measurements. I like the small Dividers, shown in the center, for measuring eyes, nose, lips, and other details where the calipers may be too large.

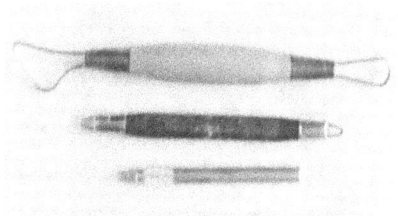

Loop End tools also come in a variety of sizes and shapes. I especially like the smallest one at the bottom as it can get into small spaces without gouging out too much clay.

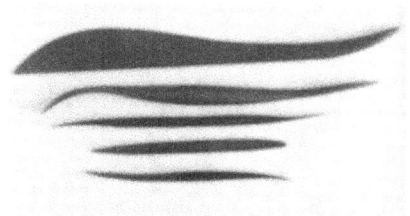

Wooden tools for working with earth clay. I prefer the hardwoods; they cost more to start with but last forever if you take care of them. Wash them, apply a generous coating of olive oil, wait a few minutes and buff off any residue. The smallest one was a gift to me in 1989 from a Master Sculptor in Germany. The curve just fits my fingers and I use it every time I sculpt.

Rubber and metal scrapers are used to smooth clay, a plastic credit card works too. Sheetrock sanding paper, bottom center, is good to take down high spots as clay begins to dry. It can scratch polymer clay, however, so use light pressure. The steel mold tool on the left is serrated on both edges and is good for taking down 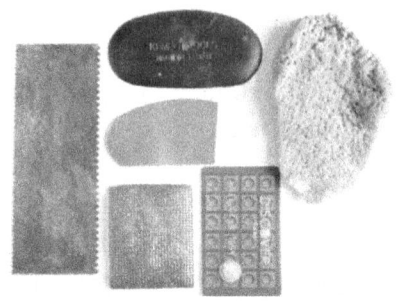 large areas on clay heads as well as plaster molds. Sponges are used for smoothing wet clay. I like Elephant Ears, they are very soft and don't leave any marks on the clay.

These stainless steel tools are for refining plaster molds but are wonderful for earth clay and polymer clay both. The serrated ones can be used to take down

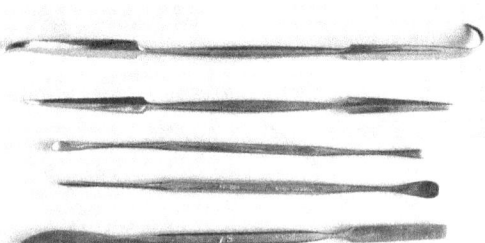

high spots on contoured areas and smooth details. They are a little expensive but well worth it. Stainless steel means easy cleanup and no problems with rust. I use these extensively.

These steel tools are similar to the stainless steel ones above and are also used for plaster work. Bigger and heavier, they come in handy for working down large clay pieces. The top five are serrated on both ends, the bottom one is smooth. The steel will rust so need a little more care. Clean and oil before you put them away.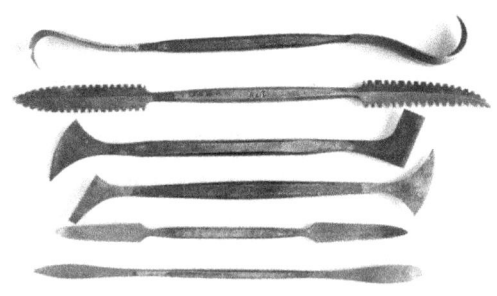

Assorted brushes, including a couple of large ones, are useful to have on hand. Soft watercolor brushes, small detail brushes and several sizes of stiff bristle brushes.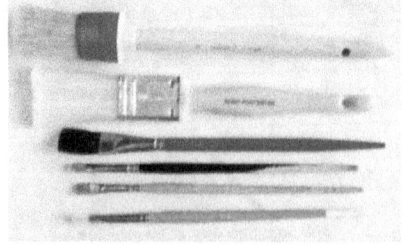

Stands

My husband makes all my sculpture and armature stands. They can be purchased but are quite easy to make and inexpensive. The base is ¾", white laminate shelving. It's easy to clean and I like the neutral color when I'm working. I have the shelving cut to 16"x16" (Figure 10-1), as that's the size of the table on my sculpting stand. Secured with C clamps, it's easy to remove and set aside if I want to work on something else. Galvanized pipe is heavy enough to support several pounds of clay and you can purchase it in different lengths to customize your stand for each project.

Supplies:
Laminate shelving, cut to desired size
2 - 1" Plumber's floor flanges
1 – 8" length of 1" galvanized pipe
1 – 1" wooden dowel approximately 12" long
Small piece of 1" wood, approximately 6"x6"
2 – C clamps (optional)
Assorted screws

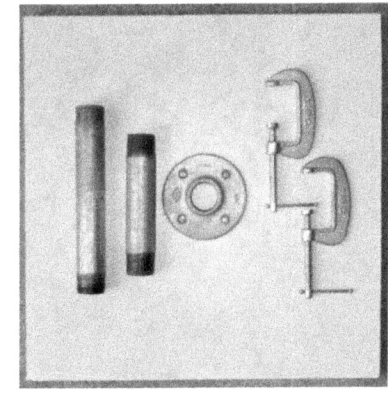

Figure 10-1

This specific stand can be used with any study skull. The wood piece is cut to fit into the under portion of the mandible. You can cut a separate piece to fit each skull you work on if desired. This takes a little trial and error to get the right shape the first time you try it, but is worth it. Turn your skull upside down and trace a pattern of the underside of the mandible onto a sheet of paper. Cut it out, test the fit, and repeat if necessary. Figure 10-3 will give you an idea of the shape of the finished piece. You can look back to Part Three, Figure 3-12, to see the underside of the mandible.

Transfer the paper pattern to the 1" piece of wood and cut it out. Test the fit on your study skull and sand the edges until it fits snugly up into the mandible. Drill a 1" hole in the center of the rounded portion of the wood. This is for the dowel to fit through.

Attach one plumber's floor flange in the center of the base. Screw the galvanized pipe into the bottom flange. The second flange is threaded onto the pipe upside down (Figure 10-2). Attach the cut out piece of wood to the flange with screws, lining up the center hole with the hole in the pipe. Drop the dowel down through the wood and the pipe (Figure 10-3). You should have about 4" of the dowel visible. The skull fits over the dowel, which will balance and support the skull so the only clay needed is to align the skull in the correct position.

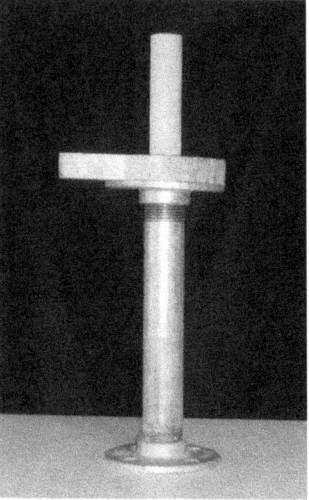

Figure 10-2

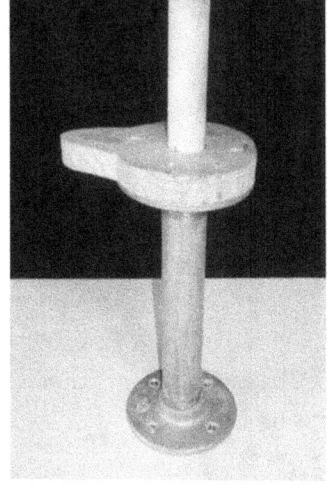

Figure 10-3

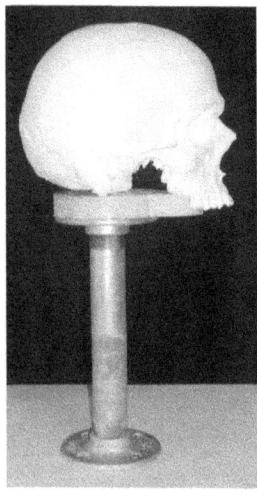

Figure 10-4

The Lower Mandible has been left off here so you can see how the cut piece of wood fits into the Upper Mandible and forms a support so it doesn't tip forward (Figure 10-4).The dowel extends up into the skull through the Foramen Magnum. Clay can be added underneath and/or to either side of the skull to bring it into the correct alignment.

I think almost all the students in my classes make this stand and are pleased with it. When not being used it breaks down and stores easily.

If you have a skull that has been cast with the cervical vertebra attached so there is no opening for the Foramen Magnum you can cut an additional piece of wood to compensate for this.

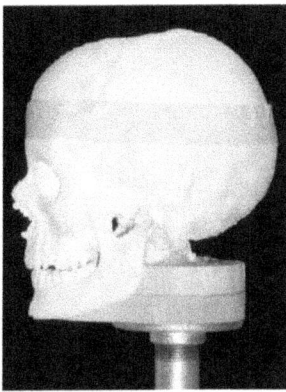

We've added a second piece of wood the same size, with a larger hole in the center (Figure 10-5). The vertebra fits down into the hole allowing the mandible to rest on the wood. Use your skull to draw a pattern so the hole is large enough for the vertebra. Secure the two pieces of wood with glue or screws.

With this modification, you can't use the center dowel to stabilize the skull; rather it is supported by the mandible resting on the wood. Use clay in and around the hole to provide additional stability and establish the correct alignment.

Figure 10-5

With this method, too much pressure against the skull might dislodge it. When adding the clay, use your other hand on the opposing side, to support the skull. Regardless of the stand you use, your study skull, or head, should be at your eye level when sculpting. Use anything available to raise your sculpture until you are looking directly into the eyes. An inexpensive plastic, rotating turn-table (the kind used for spices) lets you easily turn your sculpt to see it from all angles.

If you've taken any of my classes you know I love the give and take of questions and answers. At some point, however, a book has to end. Feel free to contact me if you have a question about something in the book.

You may know I am fascinated with the differences in ethnicities and how to portray them correctly. Look for new books on this subject in the coming year. My personal interest in age progression has led me to study the subject in depth. This is one subject that the more I learn the more I want to learn. I'd love to hear from you about what you would like to learn and how I can help you achieve your goals.

You can e-mail me, jan@windsongbooks.com, or visit the new website www.windsongbooks.com. I'll try and answer any questions that may come up.

You can also contact me through www.windsongart.com.

Glossary

Glossary

Anthropology
The study of humans and their cultures

Archaeology
Study of extinct human civilizations

Articulate
To make a joint movable – motion between two joints

Condyle
A rounded enlargement or process possessing an articulating surface

Canthus
Meeting of the upper and lower eyelids at each corner

Cranium
The portion of the skull that encloses the brain

Foramen
A hole in a bone usually for the transmission of blood vessels and/or nerves

Forensic
Pertaining to the law

Fossa
A pit or depression

Insert
To put in between

Labial
Areas nearer the lips or cheeks

Labii
Of the lip

Meatus
An opening in a bone or bony structure such as the opening for the ear, the Auditory Meatus

Origin
The fixed portion of a muscle

Ossification
The formation of bone

Osteology
The study of the structure and function of bones

Plane
A flat level surface

Prognathism
Protrusion of the jaw

Process
A general term describing any marked projection or prominence.

Skull
 The skull refers to all of the bones that comprise the head.

Soft Tissue
Muscle, tendon, ligaments, nerves, blood vessels, and fat

Superciliary
Pertaining to the eyebrows

Suture
The saw-like edge of a cranial bone that serves as joint between bones of the skull.

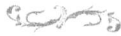

Anterior - The relative term meaning in front of, nearer the front of the body
Posterior - The relative term meaning near the rear, nearer the back of the body

Depressor - A muscle that draws down
Levator - A muscle that raises a body part

Inferior - Situated below something, or of the lower portion of the body
Superior - Situated above something, nearer the top or of the upper portion of the body

Medial - The relative term indicating a point lying nearer the mid-sagittal plane (the mid-line of the body)
Lateral - The relative term indicating a point lying farther from the mid-sagittal plane (the midline of the body)

Medial Canthus - The inner corner where the eyelids meet
Lateral Canthus - The outer corner where the eyelids meet

Proximal - A relative term indicating a point nearer the trunk, a point nearer the mid-sagittal plane (the mid-line of the body)
Distal - A relative term indicating a point that lies farther from the trunk or away from the mid-sagittal plane (the mid-line of the body)

Projecting - To jut out, or move forward
Receding - To move away or back

Projecting Zygomatic Bones -The lower portion of the zygomatic bone (the cheekbone) projects forward; Mongoloids are said to have projecting zygomatic bones. They actually drop straight down but compared to Caucasoids and Negroids they are considered projecting.

Receding Zygomatic Bones - The lower portion of the zygomatic bone (the cheekbone) projects backward; Caucasoids and Negroids have receding zygomatic bones.

Osteological Evaluation

Bone Clones ® Descriptive Analysis Report

Human, Female, White

Specimen Evaluated: Bone Clones® replica

Skeletal Inventory: 1 intact cranium
                         1 intact mandible

General observations:

In general, the molding process has preserved significant details necessary for evaluation. The general shape and configuration of the skull is within normal limits. The ectocranial morphology of the individual cranial bones is within normal limits. The sutural patterns are of expected configuration: there is the suggestion of a subtly persistent mendosal suture line at the right lateralmost extents of the occipital bone. There is the suggestion of a small sutural bone (Wormian ossicle) at the right asterion. The foramina are of expected configuration. The skull is atraumatic.

Dentition:

There are 16 teeth in the maxillary arcade and 16 teeth in the mandibular arcade. All teeth have an adult morphology and no deciduous dentition remains. The dentition is atraumatic. There are no dental restorations or prostheses. There is a moderate degree of attrition.

Features of Race:

The interocular distance is not prominently widened. The nasal root is prominent and the nasal angle is acute. The zygomatic bones retreat posteriorly from the plane of the face. The nasal aperture is narrow superiorly and broader inferiorly. The anterior nasal spine is somewhat prominent, and the inferior margin of the nasal aperture has a sharp (nasal) sill. The maxillary dental arcade is somewhat V-shaped. There is no alveolar prognathism. The maxillary incisors are blade-like. There is no edge-on-edge incisal bite. There is a slight post-bregmatic depression. The calvarial sutures are predominantly simple.

The totality of features is most in keeping with those of a White individual.

Osteological Evaluation page 2

Bone Clones ® Descriptive Analysis Report

<u>Features of Sex</u>:

There is no significant prominence of the cranial sites for musculofascial attachment. There is very slight prominence of:

- the nuchal lines
- the external occipital protuberance
- the supraorbital tori

There is a somewhat broad ascending mandibular ramus. The nasion is smooth, and the supraorbital margins are blunted. The inferior border of the mandible is rounded.

The totality of features is most in keeping with female sex.

<u>Features of Age</u>:

There are no identifiable fontanelles. The spheno-occipital synchondrosis is fused.

The sum of scores for the cranial vault (landmarks 1 through 7) is 10. This corresponds to an estimated age of 39.4 +/- 9.1 years.

The sum of scores for the anterior cranium (landmarks 6 through 10) is 11. This corresponds to an estimated age of 56.2 +/- 8.5 years.

All 32 teeth are fully erupted, and no deciduous dentition remains. There is a moderate degree of attrition on the occlusal surfaces of the dentition

<u>SUMMARY</u>:

1. White.

2. Female.

3. 47.7 – 48.5 years; range 30.3 – 64.7 years.
   a. The very narrow age estimate should not be interpreted as being precise. It is a mathematical artifact subsequent to the fact only one method of age evaluation was utilized, and the limitations of that method itself.

4. No evidence of trauma.

5. No evidence of significant osteologic variations or primary pathology.

References

Further Reading

References and Further Reading

It would be impossible to list all of the books, articles, journals and other material I've read on the subject of sculpting, forensics, and facial reconstruction over the years. I've listed a few that will get you started on the journey. You can locate others through your local library.

Bass, Bill and Jefferson, Jon "*Beyond the Body Farm: A Legendary Bone Detective Explores Murders, Mysteries, and the Revolution in Forensic Science*" (Harper Collins 2007)

Edwards, Betty "*Drawing on the Artist Within*" (Simon & Schuster Inc. 1986)

Ekman, Paul "*Emotions Revealed*" (New York: Times Books 2003)

Faigin, Gary "*The Artist's Complete Guide to Facial Expression*" (Watson-Guptill Publications/New York 1990)

Foster, Walter "*Anatomy*" (Foster Art Service, Inc. Laguna Beach, CA.)

Gibson, Lois "*Forensic Art Essentials: A Manual for Law Enforcement Artists*" (Elsevier Inc. 2008)

Gill, George and Rhine, Stanley "*Skeletal Attribution of Race and Methods for Forensic Anthropology*" (Maxwell Museum of Anthropology 2004)

Gordon, Louise "*How to Draw the Human Head*" Techniques and Anatomy (Penguin Books 1977)

Gray, Henry "*Anatomy of the Human Body*" (Lea & Febiger 1918)

Ross, Ann H, and Williams, Shanna E. "*Craniofacial Growth, Maturation, and Change: Teens to MidAdulthood*" Journal of Craniofacial Surgery 2010: 21 (2)

Hamm, Jack "*Cartooning The Head & Figure*" (Putnam Publishing Group 1967)

Jarrasse, Dominique "*Rodin*" (Finest SA / Editions Pierre Terrail Paris Italy 2001)

Lanteri, Edward *"Modeling And Sculpting The Human Figure"*
(Dover Publications, Inc. 1965)

Loomis, Andrew *"Drawing the Head"*
(Viking Press 1943)

Loomis, Andrew *"Figure Drawing for All It's Worth"*
(Viking Press 1943)

Luchessi, Bruno *"Modeling the Head in Clay"*
(Watson-Guptill Publications/New York 1979)

Luchessi, Bruno *"Terracotta, The Technique of Fired Clay Sculpture"*
(Watson-Guptill/New York 1977)

Manhein, Mary H. *"The Bone Lady"*
(Baton Rouge: LSU Press 1999)

Nafte, Myriam *"Flesh and Bone: An Introduction to Forensic Anthropology"*
(Carolina Academic Press 2009)

Peckmann, Tanya R. Saint Mary's University (Halifax, Canada); Mary Manhein,
Louisiana State University; Ginesse Listi, Louisiana State University; Michel
Fournier, RCMP, Forensic Facial Identification Services (Fredericton, Canada)
"Tissue Depth of Native Canadian Americans" (awaiting publication)

Prag, John and Neave, Richard *"Making Faces"*
(Texas A&M University Press College Station 1997)

Reed, Walt *"The Figure"* An Approach to Drawing & Construction
(North Light Books 1976)

Rhine, Stanley *"The Bone Voyage"*
(University of New Mexico Press 1998)

Salmon, Jamie Avatar Sculpture Works Unit 7 - 2760 Aberdeen Avenue,
Coquitlam BC Canada V3B 1A3 www.avatarsculptureworks.com

Sokoll, Gary *"The Art of Facial Reconstruction"*
(Pretty Good Publishers 1998)

Taylor, Karen T. *"Forensic Art and Illustration"*
(CRC Press LLC 2001)

Wilkinson, Caroline *"Forensic Facial Reconstruction"*
(Cambridge University Press 2004)

Online suppliers for study skulls

These are not listed in any particular preference, and are not the only on-line suppliers. I suggest you spend some time looking over all of them before you place an order. Study skulls may have the mandible attached with a spring so you can see the action of the jaw. Others may come with the mandible separate and you will glue it together. In this case, it will be fixed while you're working.

http://www.anatomical.com

http://www.anatomywarehouse.com

http://www.boneclones.com

http://www.boneroom.com

http://www.boneroom.com/casts/humanskullcast.html

On-line suppliers for tools

http://www.sculpt.com
http://www.sculpturehouse.com
http://www.dickblick.com

Educational and quantity discounts are available through the publisher.

www.windsongbooks.com